SNAPSHOTS OF
HOPE

Stories from
Our Family Scrapbook

SNAPSHOTS OF
HOPE

Stories from
Our Family Scrapbook

RICHMOND WEBSTER

morehouse

HARRISBURG • LONDON

Unless otherwise indicated, biblical quotations are from the New Revised Standard Version Bible, copyright 1989, Division of Christian Education of the National Council of the Churches of Christ in the United States of America. Used by permission. All rights reserved.

Morehouse Publishing, P.O. Box 1321, Harrisburg, PA 17105

Morehouse Publishing, The Tower Building, 11 York Road, London SE1 7NX

Morehouse Publishing is a Continuum imprint.

Cover design by Brenda Klinger

Library of Congress Cataloging-in-Publication Data

Webster, Richmond.
  Snapshots of hope : stories from our family scrapbook / Richmond Webster.
    p. cm.
  ISBN 0-8192-2206-2 (pbk.)
  1. Hope—Religious aspects—Christianity—Sermons. 2. Episcopal Church—Sermons. 3. Sermons, American. 4. Christian life—Anecdotes. I. Title.
  BV4638.W33 2005
  252'.03—dc22

                              2005000999

Printed in the United States of America

05 06 07 08 09   10 9 8 7 6 5 4 3 2 1

In Memory of

Ted Copeland
A man who loved snapshots

CONTENTS

FOREWORD

For some time now I have felt great warmth for Rich Webster for the very special reason that he has brought healing and hope back to a parish that I loved and served more than thirteen years, after it went through a painful period of transition. It was not until I read this collection of his stories, however, that I understood more fully one of the secrets of his impact on this congregation.

Rich Webster is a truly gifted Episcopal priest and an exceptionally fine preacher. I say this for a variety of reasons. First, he understands the narrative character of the human intellect, and he believes this can be conveyed through the power of story-telling. As you will sense as you move through these pages, he obviously has read widely and "has a nose" for a telling anecdote.

In addition, he is not afraid to dip into his own experiences and move alongside us in an authentic confessional way. One of the things that Jesus asked of his followers was to become "witnesses" to each other, and Rich Webster has fulfilled this mandate with great skill. It is clear to me that what he offers as a gift to others is not just secondhand theory that is merely an echo of what others think, but rather, truth that has first "spoken home" to his own heart and thus is worthy to be shared generously with others. His hope of these words being a blessing to his readers is rooted in the experience of their having first blessed him.

Another reason for commending these stories is their unique relevance for the culture of the twenty-first century. I am thinking here particularly of the brevity of each of these chapters. It is a well-known fact that television has had a significant impact on the attention span of almost everyone in this country. Most of us are now conditioned to the twelve minutes between commercials, which means that the capacity to stay with a sermon or a chapter in a book has been greatly reduced for many people. One of Rich Webster's shining characteristics is the succinct way that he makes his points and the commendable conciseness of his language. I find him to be wonderfully relevant to the shape of our present era.

In my mind, the essence of good preaching and storytelling has always been building a bridge between the ancient text and the lives of people in the present. The stories that make up this volume are beautiful examples of such an art. The expressions of Holy Scripture come alive in the way that Rich Webster handles them. They cease to be just words written long ago and become vital events for the here and now. I am honored and delighted to have a part in bringing these stories to a wider audience than the parish of Saint Luke's Episcopal Church in Birmingham, Alabama. What they have already accomplished there will undoubtedly happen again and again to those who read this volume. The journey before you promises to be a significant one indeed.

John R. Claypool
Former Rector of Saint Luke's Episcopal Church,
Birmingham, Alabama
Professor of Homiletics at McAfee School of Theology,
Atlanta, Georgia

INTRODUCTION

A friend of mine once told me a story about his grandmother. He grew up in a huge family with lots of cousins, and on those occasions when they gathered for family reunions, one basic rule was understood: Every child was required to line up and give a ritual kiss to grandma; afterward, they were free to ignore her for the rest of the day. This was my friend's earliest memory of his grandmother: regal but ignored, propped up in the corner while the rest of the world buzzed all around.

My friend was a young man when he was asked to help move his grandmother from her apartment to an assisted-living facility, and when he began packing the contents of her closet, he came across an old box. It was full of dusty photographs and letters, ticket stubs and playbills, poems and stories, and memorabilia from around the world. On top of this pile was a yellowed photo of a man in uniform—it was his grandfather, and underneath were passionate letters from a young man at war writing to his bride. Hours passed while my friend sat on the floor, poring over his family's story. Later that day he asked his grand-mother, "Why didn't you tell us those great stories?" With a wistful little smile, she replied, "I didn't tell you because you never asked me."

My friend's recollection came to mind because I have been thinking about the Bible these days. To be specific, I have been thinking about how we read the Bible and how our reading it shapes the way we live out our Christian faith and life. I first had these thoughts while serving as a minister in a small town in north Alabama. Our congregation was an old "downtown church," within several city blocks of other old "downtown churches." And while we shared much the same language, much the same architecture, much the same traditions and holidays, there were also marked differences between the communities. For instance, one of these churches allowed no instrumental music, whereas my own church boasted a fine pipe organ. A couple of these other churches didn't allow women to serve as ordained ministers, whereas my denomination has ordained women for years. For many of these churches, only mature believers are welcome for baptism, whereas in my church, families often brought their babies for baptism. The list goes on, but for now I will submit that the foundation of our difference lies in our own basic understanding of the Bible and the role it has in shaping our Christian faith and life.

Of course, our differences go beyond the ways churches merely behave. In fact, I wonder whether Christian people actually spend a great deal of time talking right past one another when it comes to the Bible. For instance, our part of the country, the Bible Belt, has seen the rise of many "Christian academies" and volumes of home-school curricula intended to safeguard against "scientific theories" of creation. And yet, there are Christian people who are also scientists and have no problem holding the book of Genesis in one hand and various evolutionary theories in the other. Who is right? Are science and knowledge really a threat to faith?

Another example seems to happen every fall as we begin a new Sunday school year in the church. Someone will invariably ask why we don't teach more *Bible* to our children. I try to point out that we do teach lots of Bible, and in fact our own liturgy contains great chunks of scripture every Sunday morning. But their request has more to do with Bible geography—getting the book in order, memorizing verses and chapters—than anything else. I can certainly understand the request, but I wonder whether learning the location of Nehemiah or Philemon is as fundamentally important as discovering what these texts might actually say to us.

All this brings me back to my thoughts concerning the Bible and what we actually do with it. If the Bible is only a book of rules and regulations, a reference book, or a playbook (one friend calls the Bible his "owner's manual"), then we might do well to memorize the order of books or key verses that guide our lives. If the Bible is an encoded prediction of the end of the world, then we might do well to study the imagery of Daniel or Revelation or study and watch the popular books and movies from this perspective. If it is a science book, then secular theories and new discoveries may well be a threat. If it is a musty old relic with little to do with "real life," then we might do well to prop it up in the corner like an ancient relative and offer it our ritual kiss.

Still, I wonder whether there might not be another way to spend time with this book, to love this book, to "read, mark, learn, and inwardly digest"[1] this book and let it speak to our everyday lives. As it is really not a book at all, but rather a library of texts encompassing many different voices from across many different centuries, I wonder if we can't begin to discover the Bible in much the same way as my friend discovered his grandmother's stories. We can imagine the Bible as a scrapbook—a big old family scrapbook with poems, letters, history, humor, and tragedy—all snapshots of our family story.

The following pages are basically this scrapbook theory put into practice. Scripture passages have become "snapshots," with stories chosen alongside in an attempt to reflect the truth of the passage or unveil its meaning. To be honest, the more time I spend with this idea, the more it seems to fit. Like any old scrapbook we might find sitting on our parents' coffee table, this collection is chock-full of pictures. Snapshots beget snapshots until, when we open the book, there is no telling what might fall out! Some images may seem incongruous at first, yet I like to think it works as a whole since, as in most family scrapbooks (and in families themselves), one still finds a common thread. The thread binding all these stories is hope, grounded in the ever-present reality of God.

My hope and prayer is that as you read these stories, you will begin to find a few stories of your own—stories that strengthen your faith, stories that remind you of what is real, stories that inspire you to dig out that family scrapbook we call the Bible and curl up for a good read.

NOTE

1. Book of Common Prayer (New York: The Church Hymnal Corporation, 1979), 184.

CHAPTER 1

GRATITUDE AND HOPE

A snapshot of relationship

Then the Father said to him, "Son, you are always with me, and all that is mine is yours. But we had to celebrate and rejoice, because this brother of yours was dead and has come to life; he was lost and has been found."

Luke 15:31–32

Not too long ago, something happened out of the blue that I don't think I will ever forget. It was a Monday morning, and I was taking the church deposit to the bank downtown, when a voice from the parking lot stopped me short: "Pastor, will you come pray with me?"

Now before I go any further, I want to tell you that there definitely are pitfalls to wearing a clerical collar in the Bible Belt. I've seen it all—the concerned faces of restaurant patrons as I sit with my wife at lunch ("Will that be separate checks, Father?"); the hush as I enter a room and realize that I am either missing out on a really good story or scaring someone half to death. Just the other day, I was riding on a crowded elevator in the hospital when an orderly stepped in. He recognized a colleague standing next to me and said cheerfully, "Girlfriend, where have I seen you before?" His friend glanced sideways at me before saying, "I'll have to tell you later."

All this is to say that a minister's clerical collar can be a magnet for all sorts of adventures and mishaps. But sometimes being recognized as a minister on the street is pure grace. This was one of those times. We sat together on a low wall next to the front door while the man told me of his predicament. It was a story almost too sad to tell. He was an old black gentleman, the red dirt on his trousers and shirt suggesting he made his living on the land. He held a carefully folded bandanna that was soaked with his own tears, and he shook softly as he began: "Pastor, I got a bad cancer, and the doctor says I got months to live." We stayed there for a little while, talking about faith, family, and the promises of God. This man was clearly a Christian. He was afraid, to be sure, but he also knew the Lord and had no doubt that God was with him, even here in the valley of the shadow of death.

I took his hand, and offered a prayer. It wasn't much, just a little prayer for the journey. Episcopal clergy aren't known for their extemporaneous prayer skills, and this morning there wasn't a prayer book for miles. Still, we were clearly on Holy Ground, and I will never forget his soft refrain to my own prayer, "Yes Lord; thank you, Jesus; thank you."

It has been said that the world is hard on those who have to live in it, and that morning I realized nothing else I had planned for the day seemed all that important by comparison—not the bank deposit, or the post office, or the cares of the day. In some mysterious way, our time together had been a gift, a reminder to us both of what it means to be in relationship with the same God who made us, knows us, and calls us by name. After all, our journey with God is not about pious platitudes or fancy prayers, stained glass or Sunday ritual. The old man's refrain stands in my memory as witness to life lived in gratitude and hope—gratitude for the gifts of God, even when life doesn't work out like we had wished or planned, and the unfailing hope that God always keeps his promises.

This snapshot from the fifteenth chapter of Luke is one of the best-known and best-loved stories in all of scripture. Like the man in the parking lot, it, too, is a reminder of our need to be in relationship with God, though I wonder if it is a story we know so well that we hardly know it at all. Put another way, I wonder if we ever pause to consider that this is more than a story about a boy who sowed his wild oats before returning home. I wonder if we can we read it as a story about us and consider our own relationship with God—even when things haven't turned out quite like we wished or planned.

This parable is special to me, since I had my own little adventure in learning its meaning. As a seminary student, I was struggling to write a sermon based on this story when a very wise teacher sent me on a little field trip. She told me to go to the National Gallery, across the river in Washington, DC, and find a painting by the seventeenth-century Spaniard Bartolomé Murillo titled *Return of the Prodigal.* If you have ever seen it, I'm sure you will agree that it is breathtaking. To begin with, the painting is huge, more than six feet tall, and it is full of rich detail. The composition centers on a benevolent father embracing an emaciated son. They are accompanied by a servant bearing a ring on a pillow, while another leads in a fatted calf. A little dog was even added to the composition, leaping and barking as the ultimate welcome home.

I wrote down everything I saw and called my teacher. After I finished with my description, she asked, "Now read the parable again, and tell me what you *didn't* see in the painting." Her point was crystal clear. For all his detail, Murillo had left out the older brother. He only told *half* the story. "There was a man who had two sons," the story begins, but all too often we stop with the boy who returned home.

Who could blame Murillo? The story of the older brother is almost too sad to tell. He was in the field working when his brother finally returned, so he didn't even know what had happened until he heard music coming from the house. It was a servant who finally broke the news that his brother was safe at home again and his father had thrown the boy a party. But he couldn't join them. He couldn't go in. He just couldn't imagine how things had turned out for his little brother. As far as he was concerned, finding his brother dead was always a possibility; crawling back on his hands and knees was yet another. But he just couldn't fathom his father giving a party for someone who had squandered the family fortune and brought shame to the family name.

Of course, there was another reason he couldn't join the party, a deeper reason. He simply didn't have a relationship with his father, or anyone else, for that matter. True, he worked like a slave for the family business, but his father didn't want him to be a slave. He wanted his son to be a child. The older brother never broke a rule and he never left home, but his heart was far from home—farther than his little brother dared to go. He was so lost, he couldn't see the gifts his father gave him every day; he couldn't trust the hand of grace that would be extended to him as well. In short, he lived a life without gratitude and hope.

In the spring of 2004, my family moved from Decatur, Alabama, to the city of Birmingham. I actually moved ahead of my wife and children some months before, and though many people have stories of separation more trying than ours, I'm very glad it's over. There were times when the pain of separation was most acute—a missed choral performance, a good report card, and an injured pet all reminded me that our little family unit was broken. But I also think we can look back on that difficult time and see little gifts along the way. In fact, there were moments when we truly discovered the meaning of family.

One of these moments happened on Ellen's birthday. Anyone who knows my wife also knows that birthdays are a big deal with her. No one can stretch out a birthday like Ellen Webster. It works like this: Toward the end of April, Ellen will announce to the family that we all have to be nice to her because it is her "birthday week." She tried to stretch all this out into a month once, but we wouldn't let her get away with it. The best part of this little game is that everyone else gets the royal birthday treatment as well. On the night before each person's big day, after everyone has gone to bed, Ellen becomes the "birthday fairy," decorating the honoree's breakfast chair like a throne, complete with crepe paper, balloons, and a hat to announce the beginning of a very special day.

Now it is usually my job as a secondary or "fill-in" birthday fairy to pick up the job of decorating for Ellen's big day. But with Daddy gone, I figured we would have to suspend the tradition for that year. Ellen never complained a bit, but I also knew that she would be sad as she sat in an unadorned breakfast chair. What I hadn't counted on was the fact that our ten-year-old daughter, Betsy, had been thinking the same thing. The morning of my wife's birthday, I got a call from Ellen first. It was about 6:30 in the morning, and she had just returned from taking my son to early-morning football practice. "You aren't going to believe this," she said. "The birthday fairy came to see me." It was true. While Ellen was out running errands, Betsy got out of bed early and strung miles of crepe paper all over her mother's breakfast chair, set out a homemade card, and placed her own favorite stuffed animal as a gift in the center of the table. It was beautiful, and in the end, Betsy gave her mother something better than her favorite toy—Betsy became the birthday fairy. In fact, I don't think either parent will ever forget the day our little girl loved us enough to keep the family traditions going. Can you see it now? This is the vision of life God holds out for us. A life lived in community, a life lived in mutual understanding, a life lived in love.

I attended a conference some years ago where the speaker portrayed some of our popular images of God. He used props and hats, and it was pretty effective. First, the speaker donned a cowboy hat and brandished a toy six-gun. He was God the Divine Lawman. "Hey, you down there!" he barked. "You broke one of my commandments! Pow! You get the flu!" Next, he put on an apron and became God the Celestial Waiter, pathetically doing all he could to please in order to prove his existence. Finally, he sat in a rocking hair and became God the Old Man, continually dozing and forgetting his own name.

His performance was both hilarious and revealing. These popular notions of God—from sheriff to cosmic vending machine to grandfather—all had one thing in common: They all reveal a fundamental lack of *relationship*, and we might do well to ask ourselves if we, too, have strayed far from home. Remember, God doesn't want slaves; God wants children. God wants our hearts, not our best behavior, and he wants us together. In short, God wants to journey with us as a family—through ups and downs, through celebrations and disappointments, through triumph and tragedy. God is very near, if we only allow him to be a part of our lives. God is as close as a prayer, as close as a neighbor, as close as a wish, a dream, even a tear.

Come home and rest. Let your heavenly Father welcome you with open arms. Discover a life filled with gratitude and hope. The party is waiting. *Thank you, Jesus; thank you.*

CHAPTER 2

THE CROSSING GUARD

A snapshot of extravagant living

> *Truly I tell you, this poor widow has put in more*
> *than all those who were contributing to the treasury.*
> *For all of them have contributed out of their*
> *abundance; but she out of her poverty has put in*
> *everything she had, all she had to live on.*
>
> Mark 12:43–44

From late August until May in the city of Decatur, Alabama, a select group of fifth graders serve as crossing guards in front of their elementary schools. Rain or shine, these children keep watch as little ones pour out of their parents' cars, cross busy streets and parking lots, or wobble on their bikes in the midst of morning traffic. And while those who don the orange vests must arrive a little early for school each day, it is a job that carries with it a certain *prestige.* In fact, the children usually vie for the privilege.

As with most schools in most towns, each place has its own traditions, its own requirements when it comes to parking etiquette and expectations. Within a week of the new school year, all the parents know whether they may turn left (or not) in the parking lot. They know where to stop and where to let Junior out of the car. They know these things because even a minor infraction will bring the immediate attention of a ten-year-old carrying a flag and wearing the badge of authority. But there is another kind of crossing guard tradition unique to Decatur, an event I used to enjoy every morning along the street behind Eastwood Elementary School.

As best as I can tell, it all began when a little girl named Anna Laura was told to stand beside the crosswalk on Eastwood Drive. She was a brand-new crossing guard, and this was not really the place for her. To begin with, Anna Laura is the kind of happy, vivacious girl who greets the world with a smile every day. But this particular post was not the place for a girl with her gifts. This crosswalk was on the backside of the playground, the farthest from all the other children. At this crosswalk, there would be precious few children to greet and help across the road. At this crosswalk, there would be no car doors to open for little ones loaded down with backpacks and science fair projects. At this crosswalk, there would be nothing for her to do except stand at attention with her vest and her flag, watching the world hurry by on its way to school.

Incidentally, I'm somewhat of an expert on the subject of crosswalks, as I happen to be the parent of a former crossing guard. I also am sensitive to the injustice of Anna Laura's assignment, since my son was assigned to one of the busy (important) crosswalks, and he didn't even smile for the entire school year. Friends called him "Mr. Sunshine." Perhaps it was the weight of his responsibility. I'll have to ask. But day after day, it was always the same: Copeland simply stood on his corner, the silent lawman, impassive as a guard outside of 10 Downing Street.

Needless to say, Anna Laura was very disappointed with her assignment. But she hung in there, and in time, we all began to notice that something special was happening behind the playground on Eastwood Drive. In short, Anna Laura was merely content to stand around holding her flag. True, she couldn't open any car doors back there, or even help many children cross the road. But she could wave, and it was here that she perfected the art. She waved to everyone, and it wasn't just some little wave, some mere acknowledgment that she knew you from the neighborhood or that she happened to catch your eye. Rather, she really waved, and smiled, and leaned, and shouted greetings to anyone driving by. I remember my wife telling me about her first: "You have just got to ride down Eastwood Drive and see that cute girl waving to everybody." In time, Anna Laura became a goodwill ambassador of sorts, whether she knew it or not. Any visitor to southeast Decatur would have to conclude that East-wood School was the friendliest place in town. I even changed my morning route to work just to see her wave and start my day with a smile.

I'll say this again: Something special was happening behind the playground on Eastwood Drive, and I believe it was some-thing deeper than a little girl's greeting the world with a smile, or even making the best of a bad situation. Rather, Anna Laura became a daily reminder of what it means to live extravagantly—to never hold back, to have hope and deep joy, even when things don't work out as we might wish or plan. As far as I'm con-cerned, Anna Laura fits squarely in this snapshot from the twelfth chapter of Mark.

Jesus was teaching in the Temple in Jerusalem, and as he looked all around, he saw that the practice of their religion had fallen far short of God's plan. Temple dignitaries, and others of great wealth and importance, had turned this house of God into a mere showcase of money and power. As Jesus saw it, religion in this place had become, at best, a mere pretext for social advancement, and at worst, a rip-off scheme to oppress the poor and powerless. But all was not lost in the Temple that day, as Jesus noticed a woman enter the room. She was a poor widow, invisible in their culture, and far removed from the lives of the rich and powerful. We don't know anything more about her, but it is no stretch to imagine that her life hadn't worked out as she had ever wished or planned. But she came with a gift, and Jesus saw that something special was happening here. True, it was only a little gift—two small coins worth only a penny—yet Jesus knew something deeper was at work than the mere generosity of a woman with precious little to give.

A few years ago, I ran across a remarkable essay titled "Beneath the Surface," in which a minister, David Hansen, recalls some of the lessons he learned while working in the Alzheimer's unit of a nursing home.[1] One morning, his group began with a project in which patients were given small bags to fill with candy for an upcoming party. The minister was paired with a woman who struggled to tie ribbons around the bags of cellophane. He noticed her frustration as she tried to remember how to tie a bow. So he asked her, "How about if you hold the ribbon, and I'll tie the bow?" The woman smiled, and Hansen learned his first lesson for the day: The point of their time together had little to do with getting things done efficiently, and everything to do with enjoying each other's company.

Still, there were other lessons for the minister to learn that day. After filling the party bags, it was now time for the morning devotion. He got out his King James Bible and began slowly reading the twenty-third Psalm: "The Lord is my shepherd, I shall not . . ." He stopped before the last word. "Want!" said a few. "Good job," he said. Then he continued: "He maketh me to lie down in green . . ." "Pastures!" they replied. Everyone was into the game by now. "He leadeth me beside . . ." "Still waters!" After a while, the game began to falter a bit, so the minister decided to try something else. He began to sing verses from old hymns, and suddenly a woman called out, "I can play the piano!"

As they all sat around the upright, singing gospel hymns, the minister began to understand how God sees his children. That is, he began to see these people beneath the surface of their disease. He saw in that room that the soul of a woman who could not tell you her address or the year she was born was also the soul of a woman who played the piano for thirty years in her church. He saw that the soul of a man growling out Bible verses was also the soul of a young father teaching his children the twenty-third Psalm. He saw that the soul of a woman unable to tie a bow was also the soul of a young girl tying bows in her hair before her first date. In short, he saw them as God sees them—extravagantly. After all, though their brains may well have been hurt by this dreaded disease, their souls worked just fine. As the minister put it so eloquently: "All we have to do is hold the ribbon. God will tie the bow."

The widow's small offering, like Anna Laura's wave, was a reminder that life itself is a gift. Every day, every breath, every smile, every tear, every dream, every wave, every friend is a gift. Of all the people gathered in the Temple, the widow alone seemed to understand that. The woman simply didn't hold back, and as Jesus pointed out, her gift of two little coins was worth more than all the money in the Temple bank. Put another way, she knew what it meant to live extravagantly.

The late Fred Rogers, of *Mister Rogers' Neighborhood* fame, once wrote of visiting a little church while on a weekend vacation in New England. The service itself was okay but, as he put it, "the sermon was dreadful." Rogers was a young seminarian at the time, especially attuned to the art of preaching, and this performance was the worst he could imagine. The preacher certainly tried hard enough, but he was dull, inarticulate, and broke just about every rule that Rogers knew about good preaching. Rogers recalled that at the end of the sermon, a woman leaned over with a tear in her eye. She whispered, "He said exactly what I needed to hear." It was then that Rogers knew something special had happened in church that morning—only his pride and education had kept him from seeing it. His neighbor in the pew had come to God in need, and the preacher had done his best to share the Gospel he carried in his heart. Between the two—the one who hungered for God and the one who fed her—Rogers felt as if he had witnessed something deeper than a nice Sunday service. Rogers caught a glimpse of extravagant living. As he reflected later, "That New England Sunday experience fueled my desire to be a better neighbor wherever I am."[2] Of course, the rest is history. What followed for Rogers was a lifetime of extravagant love for all God's children and a television career that changed the lives of countless families forever.

I hope you will see that these stories leave us with a challenge—to live extravagantly ourselves, and to look for the gifts of God wherever we go. We know that life doesn't always work out as we might wish or plan. But if we try, I believe we can find what we all truly want: peace in our souls, deep joy, genuine satisfaction, and a quiet mind. Who knows? Perhaps with God's help, we can share these things with others and heal this broken world.

Anna Laura left her spot on Eastwood Drive in the spring. That year, like all years when our children are young, passed too quickly. Anna Laura graduated, and a new crossing guard was put in place. But the wave remains, and to this day, if you drive along the backside of the playground, someone will be there to make your day. Look around, and pass on the gift.

NOTES

1. David Hansen, "Beneath the Surface," *Christianity Today/International Leadership Journal* 21, no. 2 (Spring 2000): 116.

2. Fred Rogers, *The World According to Mr. Rogers* (New York: Hyperion, 2003), 126.

CHAPTER 3

WHAT ARE WE LOOKING FOR IN THE FIRST PLACE?

A snapshot for those who want to be disciples

> *Jerusalem, Jerusalem, the city that kills the prophets and stones those who are sent to it! How often have I desired to gather your children together as a hen gathers her brood under her wings, and you were not willing!*
>
> Luke 13:34

One of the Big Events in our family history has to be the day the Webster family got a dog. Now this might not seem like such a big deal for many, but for us the decision was huge. I had put this off for a long time, in spite of the begging and pleading from my children, in spite of the unbearable shame they felt every day for not being dog owners. My reasons were sound: First of all, we didn't have a fence, so an outside dog was out of the question. As for an inside dog, well, my wife, Ellen, is the kind of woman who goes through life with a bottle of Fantastik® in one hand and a bottle of Murphy's Oil Soap in the other.

But I finally gave in, and we got a dog. It happened this way: A week or so before the Big Decision, my mother-in-law saw an ad for a dog in the Montgomery newspaper. This was not just any dog, but a Yorkshire terrier—to her the most noble breed on earth. This was the dog she wanted my children to have for their birthdays the next month, and she was even willing to foot part of the bill, which brings me to another reason we couldn't have a dog. Dogs are expensive, but Yorkies are very expensive, and even with my mother-in-law going in for half, I couldn't imagine working a fancy little British dog into our budget. "No problem," she said. This dog was only a $100, a steal by Yorkie standards, and the dog's owners lived just up the road in Athens. She was an adult dog—good for the kids, my mother-in-law assured us—and it would be her treat. So the next Sunday afternoon, we drove north to get our dog.

I will never forget our children's faces when we told them. It was our lucky day, and on the way up we decided to name her Lucky. We all imagined what life would be like with our new dog. Betsy imagined combing her coat, sleeping with her in the bed. Copeland imagined romping with her in the front yard. Ellen imagined her being house-trained, and I even got into the game a bit—I imagined a richly appointed room, with tapestries and oriental rugs. I'm wearing a smoking jacket, and I have a fancy little dog in my lap . . .

We finally reached our destination, and the children piled out of the car. A man came to the door, and we identified ourselves as the proud new owners of his dog. Wordless, he ambled down to the kennel behind the house. His wife walked up, and while we waited, she began to list all the things we would need to buy, all the shots the dog didn't have. The man finally returned, holding what had to be the filthiest dog I have ever seen. She hung like a limp rag, and he thrust the little animal toward my son. "Dog stinks," he said and walked away.

We stood in a circle, looking at our new dog. There was no going back now. The children would see to that. The dog didn't seem all that glad to see us and even tried to bite Ellen. I paid the woman, and we exchanged looks—and I will never forget the look on her face that seemed to say, "Hey, big spenders, what in the world were you looking for?" That night, as Ellen and I bathed our little dog in the bathtub, my wife looked down at the filthy water, the quivering animal, and said, "Well, Rich, it looks like we got ourselves a hundred-dollar Yorkie."

Needless to say, things can turn out differently than we might expect or assume, and it sure helps to know what you are looking for in the first place, which is precisely the point of this snapshot from the thirteenth chapter of Luke. After all, we are not told how the disciples felt as they heard Jesus weeping over Jerusalem that day, but it is no stretch to imagine that this prediction was very different than any of them expected or assumed. Up to that point, they had followed Jesus through all sorts of adventures. They watched him heal the sick, feed the hungry, calm a storm, even raise the dead. Crowds followed them everywhere, so they even enjoyed a little celebrity status to boot.

By the time we reach the thirteenth chapter of Luke, they have begun a long journey to Jerusalem, a journey no doubt expected to bring more fame, more power, more recognition than ever before. But forces were already conspiring against them, forces that Jesus knew would spell their doom. No one else may have seen it coming, but Jesus knew all too well that this journey would end in betrayal, rejection, and death. In short, we may never know what the disciples were looking for when they first signed on with Jesus, but here we learn that it was going to be risky to follow Jesus into the city that kills its prophets.

That said, it is still hard for us to fully appreciate the impact of the story. It may have been dangerous for them, but these days we rarely feel persecuted for our faith, outside the occasional risk of social suicide. But we can read lessons like these and remember Christians in the world who know all too well how Jesus felt that day. There are Christians who fully know the cost of the journey.

I met a priest from the region of southern Sudan during my seminary days. We sat together during lunch one day, and when I asked about his family and his church, he told me a story I never expected to hear. His people had suffered under government-sponsored terrorism for years. Christians were an open and easy target in this predominantly Muslim country, and recently his village had been burned. In fact, his people—family, friends, neighbors, the entire congregation—were gone somewhere, and he didn't know exactly where they were. I sat in stunned silence, trying to fathom the cost of discipleship for the people of his country. But then the priest added, with a wry smile, "We may be on the run, but our church still has an evangelism committee."

And why would he say that? Why would they invite others to join them on this journey? Because they know something that Jesus knew that day as he looked down the road to Jerusalem. They know, deep in their bones, that in spite of all appearances to the contrary, in spite of shattered dreams and expectations, in spite of pain and fear and death itself, God wins.

I believe this leaves us with an important question, especially for churchgoing folks: What are we looking for, Sunday after Sunday, when we come to church? Are we looking for a beautiful service, a nice place for the kids, a quiet moment, a chance to see friends and family? All of these are good things, and membership does have its privileges. They tell a funny little story down at Saint John's Episcopal Church in Montgomery about an elderly parishioner who was in the hospital in Houston, Texas. A local priest stopped by to visit the woman in her hospital room and asked if he could offer a prayer. She replied, "No thanks, they are praying for me at Saint John's."

Now I think this is a charming sentiment, but I also believe we are selling God a little short if all we expect from church is a community of the like-minded. We are missing the point if we assume God just wants us here for a little "R and R." I wonder what would happen if we came together on a Sunday morning sometime expecting to hear a word from the Lord, looking for signs that tell us that God wins, or seeking to follow Jesus—wherever he might lead us? I wonder . . .

Novelist and culture critic James Carroll writes of a trip he took to Jerusalem as a young seminarian.[1] He made his pilgrimage with the idea of finding inspiration but instead found himself, initially at least, deeply disappointed. Shouldering his way among crowds of tourists and fellow pilgrims, Carroll felt that the commercial phoniness and petty worldliness of the place obscured what could have been holy about the land where Jesus walked. In fact, it wasn't long before he felt distant from the very God he sought in the first place. Entering the Church of the Holy Sepulcher—revered as the sight of the empty tomb of Jesus—he found nothing to recognize from scripture. Instead, he found a cluttered and crumbling church, the scene of a centuries-old fight for space between rival Christian groups. Even as he entered the dark cell beneath the church that is said to be the tomb itself, Carroll found it wasn't empty at all. A monk was waiting there to thrust a candle his way and demand a dollar for it.

And yet, he did find the inspiration he sought, though it wasn't among the trinkets and crowds of Jerusalem. Instead, he found what he was seeking in a hole in the ground. An archaeologist friend took him one day to a dig deep beneath the street of the Old City. The air inside was dank, and a string of light-bulbs hung from a wire suspended along the wall. At Carroll's feet lay a stone slab. "This was the threshold of the city gate at the time of Jesus," his friend told him. "It was buried in rubble for almost two thousand years and is just now being uncovered. It is certain that Jesus of Nazareth would have stepped on this stone as he left the city for Golgotha." Carroll's response was automatic. He fell to his knees and kissed the rock. Here, there were no obstacles or distractions or cheesy trinkets. Here, he could touch what Jesus touched. Here, he could feel close to the One who crossed this very threshold on the way to his death. Here, he could worship the One who rose again and left the tomb empty. Here.

This much we know: If finding Jesus is hard enough with all the distractions and barriers of this world, then following Jesus is also risky business. Our Gospel tells us to count on it. Even if we never suffer from physical danger like the people of southern Sudan, we still might find the Christian life more challenging than we ever imagined. After all, following Jesus might lead us into places that are unfamiliar or uncomfortable. Following Jesus might require us to swallow our pride or give up our control. Following Jesus might require us to forgive an enemy or learn that we are not the center of the universe. But if we only try, we might just discover that it is the best way to live. Remember, God wants a relationship with all of us. God wants to heal our hurts, feed our souls, save us from death. All we have to do is follow, and if we refuse, we may as well ask ourselves what we were looking for in the first place.

By the way, we didn't keep the dog. And I never bought that smoking jacket. In the end, it turned out that Lucky didn't like us any better than we liked her. Still, God is patient with his children and good to all his beloved creatures, great and small. We found a new home for Lucky in Montgomery, and about a month later, we brought home a dog from the animal shelter—a little mixed-breed. He plays with Copeland, he sleeps with Betsy, and we all think he is the most noble breed on earth—which was what we were looking for in the first place.

NOTE

1. James Carroll, *Constantine's Sword* (New York: Houghton Mifflin Co., 2001), 96.

CHAPTER 4

CLARITY

A snapshot of reality

*Now about eight days after these sayings Jesus
took with him Peter and John and James, and
went up on the mountain to pray. And while he
was praying, the appearance of his face changed,
and his clothes became dazzling white. Suddenly
they saw two men, Moses and Elijah, talking to
him. They appeared in glory and were speaking
of his departure, which he was about to accom-
plish at Jerusalem. Now Peter and his compan-
ions were weighed down with sleep; but since they
had stayed awake, they saw his glory and the two*

> *men who stood with him. Just as they were leav-*
> *ing him, Peter said to Jesus, "Master, it is good for*
> *us to be here; let us make three dwellings, one for*
> *you, one for Moses, and one for Elijah"—not*
> *knowing what he said. While he was saying this,*
> *a cloud came and overshadowed them; and they*
> *were terrified as they entered the cloud. Then*
> *from the cloud came a voice that said, "This is*
> *my Son, my Chosen; listen to him!" When the*
> *voice had spoken, Jesus was found alone. And*
> *they kept silent and in those days told no one any*
> *of the things they had seen.*

Luke 9:28–36

Clarity: n. The quality or state of being clear (*Webster's New Collegiate Dictionary*).

Throughout the fall of 1999, newspaper headlines told the story of Princeville, North Carolina, a town that many were calling a "waterlogged Pompeii."[1] Situated on a dangerous floodplain, Princeville literally vanished on the night of September 19 when Hurricane Floyd struck the Atlantic coast. For a time, locals feared their town would stay underwater forever. But eleven days later, the waters receded, and the people of Princeville were left to face an uncertain future. To begin with, it was a scene of utter devastation. Many houses (or what was left of them) were off their foundations and scattered across the neighborhood. Strips of insulation hung from trees, and severed power lines lay in the streets. Furniture, appliances, pictures, children's toys, books—you name it—were strewn across lawns. Mud was everywhere. Wild dogs roamed from house to house, rummaging through garbage and feeding on the carcasses of dead livestock. Even the air was marked by the flood, heavy with the stench of death and broken septic tanks.

Needless to say, the town of Princeville was completely abandoned in those days. Well, almost completely abandoned. At the far end of town, one old man remained. Not that this was easy for him, mind you—mud and debris covered his house, and gaping holes let in the wind and rain. He had no electricity, no water, no sewage, but the man remained. For about four months, he could be found just about anywhere amid the ruined streets of Princeville, but mostly he just stayed put, perched atop an old recliner sitting in the driveway and slowly reading his Bible. He was the town's sole inhabitant, but he hadn't always been there. On the night the floodwaters broke through the dike and covered Princeville, he joined his neighbors and others in a giant displacement camp some twenty miles west of town. But he wasn't happy. The camp was noisy, it was cramped, it was cold, and sometime in early October, the old man decided to go back home.

Meanwhile, a drama of sorts began unfolding in the displacement camp. A massive buyout had been proposed by the Federal Emergency Management Agency (FEMA). It was an all-or-nothing arrangement: Everybody stayed or everybody left. There had been so many floods in the past that no partial deals were offered this time. I guess the government figured that if FEMA would be spending millions of dollars on Princeville, they wanted the situation fixed once and for all. As town officials bickered over whether to accept the deal, attention turned to the old man who wouldn't leave his home. Slowly, steadily it dawned on others to follow the old man's lead. The future of Princeville was becoming clear. They would all go home. Make no mistake, a buyout would be easier—much easier than putting more dirt on the dike and rebuilding the town. But a buyout would separate them forever. A buyout would end a hundred years of history together. The old man and his Bible taught them this much—that beneath the mud and the filth lay their homes, their history, their heritage. Even with the challenges that lay ahead, they would not give up on Princeville. They could see now that leaving home was not an option. As the town commissioner put it simply: "We are Princeville. Princeville is our family. Princeville holds us together."

When I look at this snapshot from the Gospel of Luke, it occurs to me that Peter, John, and James could have felt a lot like the people of Princeville as they walked down that mountain together. It's a weird story, to be sure, and I think it is safe to say that though they all had seen some pretty amazing things, nothing could have prepared them for the light and the cloud, the appearance of the prophets, the change in Jesus, or the voice of God himself. And then, just like that, it was over. They were alone again, and it was time to join the others. And though we are told they didn't talk about it after it was over, and though the Gospel record is scant, it is no stretch to imagine they had been changed forever. They could see now. If they had ever been tempted to leave all this disciple business behind and return to their nets, now this was no option. After all, Jesus wasn't just the greatest teacher they ever heard, the greatest healer they ever saw, even the nicest man they ever imagined. Jesus was God's Son, and their lives would never be the same again.

A few summers ago, I had the pleasure of traveling to Honduras on a mission trip, and it was a real eye-opener. I returned with a deep appreciation for the things we have back home, an awareness of the basics we take for granted—potable water, a dry place to sleep, three meals a day, a trip to the doctor. One afternoon, my group was invited to tour a hospital ship docked nearby. Locals called it the "Mercy Ship," and it was nothing fancy—just an old cruise ship converted into a floating doctor's office. But what they did with that boat was nothing short of miraculous, since health care is so scarce in that part of the world. We heard plenty of stories that day, but the best of these happened when the first lady of Honduras visited the ship. It seems that the president's wife was a wildly popular woman, revered for her work among the poor and regarded as a savior of sorts after the devastation of Hurricane Mitch. On this day, the first lady not only toured the ship, but also asked if she could help by removing the bandages from the eyes of cataract patients.

People in countries like Honduras will travel on foot to see a doctor—any doctor. But something like cataract surgery was gold to them. Often people would become completely blind after years of untreated cataracts. So I had to smile that day as I imagined some local villager blinking in the sunlight and looking into the face of a smiling nurse, who was no nurse at all but rather the hero of the nation. I wonder if he felt a little like the disciples that day when they realized who Jesus really was . . .

I suppose we could just leave it at that, but there is more to these stories. True, the people of Princeville learned they could go home, and the disciples learned that Jesus was in fact the Son of God. In a sense, they are both stories about eyes being opened—about clarity and purpose. But this was only the beginning of those stories. With the gift of clarity would come new challenges, new adventures, new problems. I have friend who is a recovering alcoholic. For the past few years, she has been sober and healthy, but her first year was especially hard. In fact, she seemed to be in a foul mood every time I saw her. One day, I had the courage to ask her about it. She is a beautiful woman and had never looked better and certainly never felt better, so why the anger? Her answer was a bit of a surprise: "Rich, I just can't stand all this @#$*&^+ *clarity*."

The more I thought about her answer that day, the more it made sense to me. Her decision to fight her disease was only the beginning of her journey. Sober, she could now perceive the world around her as it really was, and she didn't like a lot of what she saw. Put another way, life didn't get a lot easier when she quit drinking. In fact, it was hard when she found out who her friends really were, and weren't. It was hard for her to learn what truly matters, and what doesn't. It was hard to let go of hard-won trophies, such as status, pride, and control. But she also knew that going back to her old life was no option. She was beginning to feel alive again, at home again, and therein lies the gift.

One afternoon, I treated myself to a little time off and caught the Winslow Homer exhibit at a local museum. It was a collection of magazine illustrations and was fascinating, not so much because of the art itself, but because the pictures were snapshots of American life before, during, and after the Civil War. By following his illustrations in sequence, one could wander through New England in the 1850s. There were scenes from the beach, of Thanksgiving celebrations, of Christmas, of a street in Boston, of ice-skating on a frozen pond. After these sweet, somewhat bucolic images came the war years, with Homer reporting from the front lines. Here, the pictures were very different. With titles such as *Bayonet Charge* or *Artillery Barrage*, these portrayed New England men and boys amid the horrors of war. Thanksgiving scenes were now beside campfires far from home. Instead of skating on frozen ponds, men huddled on frozen battlefields.

In the years following the war, it seems that Homer was asked to return to his former subjects. The museum didn't say anything about this, but my guess is that Homer's editors wanted life to return to normal for their readers as quickly as possible. There were the familiar scenes once again—young lovers walking on the beach, families skating once again at Christmas. But the famous illustrator now included new details. In one Boston street scene at Christmas, an amputee leans on crutches against a building. In another, a young father skates with his children, his left sleeve empty and pinned against his chest. In still another, a man wearing an eye patch makes a Thanksgiving toast. Obviously, things were different now. This was 1866, not 1856. So much had been destroyed; so much had been lost. Homer could see that. They could all see that. And yet, some things still endured. He could see that, too. I couldn't help thinking that this is why Homer chose to illustrate his former subjects with new clarity. I like to imagine him saying: "Life may never be the same again after this war; so many have died, and so many have suffered. But there always will be the salt spray of the coast, the smell of turkey baking in the oven, the frozen pond, the laughter of children, and Christmas."

Sunday after Sunday, I climb into the pulpit and proclaim what I know to be true about God and his children. I will usually say something like this: "Healing, forgiveness, restoration, happiness, faith, joy, and deep peace are not just a fond wish or a pipe dream, but a present reality for those who will accept it. These are the gifts of God for the people of God." But there is yet another gift. This gift is clarity. Clarity helps us understand that as Christian people, we are still a work in progress. Clarity invites us to seek the truth, whatever the cost, no matter how hard the work. Clarity prepares us for the mystery of grace.

Nobody ever said life was easy. We all make mistakes; we all have regrets. At every turn, it seems, people let us down, and others hurt us. Loved ones die, others leave, and sometimes we feel so alone. It is easy then to hide behind our fear, our anger, or our cynicism. It is easy to be mean, or sad, or mistrustful. That's what makes clarity so jarring sometimes. When God shows us the world as it really is, or himself as he really is, we might not like what we see. We might not even want to talk about it all that much. But as Christian people, we also know that quitting is not an option. That much is clear enough. If we only have the courage, like the people of Princeville, like the disciples on the mountain, like my friend who battles her alcoholism, then we too can face the future in hope, no matter how hard the work. We can listen to one another; we can heal. We can look in the mirror and see ourselves as we really are. We can look around and see our neighbors as children of God. We can hold on to the things that endure and learn what it means to be a family. We can know deep in our bones what it means to go home.

NOTE

1. Jake Helpern, *Braving Home* (New York: Houghton, Mifflin Co., 2003), 10–49.

CHAPTER 5

WHEN GOD SPEAKS

A snapshot to remind us of real burdens

He said to him, "If they do not listen to Moses and the Prophets, neither will they be convinced even if someone rises from the dead."

Luke 16:31

I am beginning to learn that when God chooses to speak to us, it usually happens in places or at times that are truly unexpected. I will never forget one of these times, since it didn't happen on a Sunday or even in church, but rather on a Tuesday night in the Wendy's on Highway 280. It had been a long day at work, a very long day, and being back in the days before my family joined me in Birmingham, I decided that my best bet for dinner would be a quick burger somewhere and an early bedtime.

It all started as I was standing in line to order. A disheveled and filthy man was causing a stir among the customers as he kept asking for a ride downtown. "*Great.* Just great," I thought. It's dark. I'm scared of downtown, and I drive a bright green Mercedes. Straight from the office, I was standing there in my clerical garb, and I knew from long experience that my uniform is a magnet for all sorts of requests, such as for handouts or rides to here and there.

Of course, I am also an easy mark. I always have been. Shortly after I was ordained and serving as a priest in Montgomery, the rector handed me a checkbook with a balance of about $2,000 and told me to go out and help the poor. I did. For the next two weeks, I became the World's Most Compassionate Preacher—I listened to hard-luck stories and wrote checks for utility bills, car repairs, bus tickets, burials, and groceries. After I ran out of money, I popped into the rector's office and asked for more. Two grand in two weeks—pretty good work, I thought. My boss shook his head and laughed. It wasn't that I was in any kind of trouble, or even that money wasn't available; it's just that he knew I would be a *marked man* from then on.

Ask anyone who knows me about my time in Montgomery, and he or she will remember lines of people waiting outside my office door, or waiting out in front of the church for my now familiar car to arrive. I became a little more savvy and discerning with time, but the reputation followed. I had the checkbook, after all. A friend made a magnet, still adorning our refrigerator, that reads: "Rich 'the Money Man' Webster: Will help you with your bills day or night. Five months' experience." My favorite story from this time came after I moved to Decatur. A woman walked into the receptionist's area, pointed to my now empty office, and asked to see the "nice preacher" (as opposed to my colleague, who was a much harder case). When the parish secretary explained that I had accepted a call to serve as rector of St. John's in Decatur, the woman was undone, exclaiming, "How am I gonna get to Decatur?"

On this night standing in Wendy's, I was not such an easy mark. I was tired and not feeling all that nice. I even tried to affect a weary look, a look that suggested to anyone who cared to notice that I had been carrying the world's burdens all day and now had punched the clock, so to speak; a look that I hoped would send the unmistakable message that this preacher was not to be bothered. I also had some hope in the arrival of a deputy sheriff, who no doubt would see that the man's needs were met—or at least scare him away.

My eyes were downcast as I found a table at which to enjoy my cheeseburger and Biggie™ fries, but I was not to dine alone. After the first bite, the man joined me. He repeated the story he already told so many times before: His car had broken down on Highway 280; he needed a ride to Fairfield, but he could get home from downtown. He asked whether I would help.

Our eyes met. He, too, had the weary look of someone carrying the burdens of the world, though his were far more of a burden than mine. After all, how can a long committee meeting even compare with a busted fuel pump on Highway 280, or feeling invisible as you ask for help again and again but to no avail? I asked him if the deputy had offered to give him a ride, and he shook his head. "That policeman wasn't no help unless I get into trouble," he said. "Then I'll get a ride downtown for sure." We both laughed at that.

And though this is hard to explain, when I looked into the man's eyes, I knew God was speaking at that moment. When I looked into the man's eyes, I knew that I was his last resort; my own surly, weary countenance ensured that. When I looked into his eyes, I knew he understood that I was also tired and more than a little afraid to give a stranger a ride downtown in the dark of night. When I looked into his eyes, I knew he understood everything. It was such a moment of mutual understanding between two of God's children that I had to look down, ashamed for having avoided him. I took another bite and had a sip of my Coke. I would give him a ride when I finished my meal.

I anticipated the next question: "Pastor, that hamburger sure does look good. You think you could buy me one?" I gave him my last $5 and told him I wanted the change. I wasn't exactly "the Money Man" that night. On the way downtown, we talked about our children and basketball, and the next morning, my car still smelled faintly of his cheeseburger with fries, a lingering reminder of my encounter with the holy.

I tell you all this because I believe there is a lesson here akin to the snapshot we find in the sixteenth chapter of Luke. I don't think Jesus told the story of the rich man and Lazarus in order to warn us about who was going to hell so much as he wanted us to know about the real burdens of this world. In other words, the rich man's problem wasn't that he was rich; his problem was that he didn't see the poor man by his gate. He was a real money man—and enjoyed all the privileges and comforts that accompany a man of his station. In his day, it was common to assume that men like him were most favored by God. It wasn't until after he died that he saw that Lazarus, poor stinky pitiful Lazarus, was most favored and much loved by God as well.

But this news was too late for the rich man. He had received all the good things he would ever get, and we can only suppose that God's generosity had reached its absolute limit. This whole situation was such an eye-opener for him that he asked if Lazarus could somehow be sent back to warn his family. But his request was denied. God tries to speak to his children every day so that we don't have to wait until we die to see the Kingdom. Besides, Moses and the Prophets and a thousand pages of scripture remind us that we ourselves are diminished when we neglect the needs of those who carry the real burdens of this world—whether begging at the gate or walking down Highway 280.

A couple years ago, newspaper headlines told of three medical missionaries (one of whom was a physician from Birmingham) who were killed by a lone gunman in the town of Jibla, Yemen. I was especially interested in the story of Bill Koehn, who kept what was pretty much the only hospital in the region open for twenty-eight years.[1] On the day of his funeral, citizens of this very Muslim country lined the streets for miles. Crowds sang, "He Is Lord" in Arabic, while others recited the Lord's Prayer. One local man reported that Koehn's death hurt him worse than the death of his own father. Outside the hospital, people gathered and wept and prayed in a ceremony normally reserved for a great leader. Only Koehn wasn't a great leader. He wasn't a scholar, or a preacher. He wasn't a doctor, or a vet, or an engineer. He was simply a grocery store manager from Kansas, a man who cared enough to share the burdens of some of the poorest people on earth.

At his memorial service in Texas, Koehn's son-in-law said: "Sometime in the future, a man will take his child to the top of a hill. He'll show him a simple marker, and he will tell his child that this man, buried all these years, brought Jesus to the backside of nowhere. And they will kneel in prayer, thanking Jesus for this saint."

In a world starved for true heroes, we marvel at stories like this. And yet, we don't have to travel to Yemen to carry on the work of the Gospel. We can do the work right here; we can share one another's burden's right here; we can follow Christ right here. This is the Kingdom, after all. God is speaking. Are we listening?

NOTE

1. *Baptist Standard*, "Just a Nobody: The Funeral Homily for Bill Koehn," January 2003.

CHAPTER 6

IN THE FAMILY

A snapshot of discipleship

After this the Lord appointed seventy others and sent them on ahead of him in pairs to every town and place where he himself intended to go. He said to them, "The harvest is plentiful, but the laborers are few; therefore ask the Lord of the harvest to send out laborers into his harvest. Go on your way. See, I am sending you out like lambs into the midst of wolves. Carry no purse, no bag, no sandals; and greet no one on the road. Whatever house you enter, first say, 'Peace to this house!' And if anyone is there who shares in peace, your

> *peace will rest on that person; but if not, it will*
> *return to you. Remain in the same house, eating*
> *and drinking whatever they provide, for the*
> *laborer deserves to be paid. Do not move about*
> *from house to house. Whenever you enter a town*
> *and its people welcome you, eat what is set before*
> *you; cure the sick who are there, and say to them,*
> *'The kingdom of God has come near to you.'"*
>
> Luke 10:1–9

In his novel *The Keys of the Kingdom* (published in 1941 and a few years later made into a movie starring a young Gregory Peck), author A. J. Cronin describes a last encounter between two men who were more brothers than friends.[1] They were an unlikely pair, one a Roman Catholic priest serving as a missionary in China, and the other a local Chinese merchant who watched the mission from a distance for more than thirty years.

Father Francis Chisholm was compassionate, open-minded, caring to all, and a problem to his superiors from day one. Because Chisholm did not appreciate the "business end" of the church, the mission he headed was considered a failure. In short, the old priest seemed content with simply living and working among the people without ever coercing them to join the mission roll. A word of explanation might help here: Long lines of desperate people appeared outside the mission door every day, and it was common to expect from these sick and hungry people at least a nominal profession of faith in return for the services provided them. This, in turn, swelled the numbers of the parish and helped with funding back home. A term was coined for these so-called converts sometime during the late nineteenth century. They were called "Rice Christians." But Chisholm would have none of that. He simply loved them all as if they were his family; he loved them without condition. The result was that after thirty years of ministry, he left a place that on paper seemed as small and insignificant as it was when he got there.

Cronin's novel, like this snapshot from the tenth chapter of Luke, stands as a reminder that the business of discipleship can be plain hard work, with little to show (on paper, anyway). To read that Jesus sent his disciples into the countryside ahead of him seems simple enough—until we consider all the places Jesus went himself. Jesus lived in a world as fragmented and polarized as our own, with deep divisions between rich and poor, educated and uneducated, healthy and sick, blessed and cursed, men and women, slave and free. You can bet his disciples didn't curry any favor with the powers that be as they went out to care for those whom the world had forgotten.

I will never forget a sermon I heard the day I graduated from seminary. It was a beautiful day, and the auditorium was filled with excited graduates, all full of knowledge and ready to take on the world as card-carrying ministers of the Gospel. I don't remember specifically what I was thinking during the service, but I was probably daydreaming about where I might put my books in the new pastor's office when the preacher suddenly brought us all back down to earth. "If you people are really good at this job," he said, "I mean really good at this, then you might just go on out there and *get yourselves killed*." Gulp. He was right, you know. It was in the Bible. Still, this vision for ministry was a little different than the one I had signed on for. What about respect, prestige, and fried chicken on Sunday?

Quite frankly, this picture from Luke offers a life that is a far cry from what the world usually expects from us. But we can also see that a miracle began to unfold as Jesus sent his friends out into the world that day, a miracle that had begun with Jesus himself, who loved tax collectors and temple priests, lepers and harlots, beggars and princes, children and old people—all in equal measure. This was what Jesus had in mind when he told his disciples to "eat what is set before you." It was more than a matter of just being respectful or polite; table fellowship was of the greatest importance in the ancient world. To eat with a person was to identify with that person, to be bound to that person, to love that person. This miracle had a name: It was the miracle of family.

A friend of mine used to tell a great story about his family. He was driving home from the beach after a long weekend of fishing with his son, when he noticed that the lights on his boat trailer weren't working properly. Ordinarily, this would be no big deal, but the man's son is autistic, and he was worried that a sudden break in routine might upset the boy. Needless to say, he was careful to explain to his son why he was pulling over to the side of the road, and that he had to check the wiring on the trailer lights because "Daddy can be so darned dyslexic sometimes."

Shortly after he pulled over, a Florida state patrolman arrived on the scene. The officer asked if he could help, and my friend suggested that he sit in the cab of the truck and press the brake pedal, adding, "Don't mind my son; he's *autistic*." The officer was understanding and kind, and he greeted the boy when he got behind the wheel. The boy leaned over and said, "Don't mind my father; he's *dyslexic*."

It has been said, and I agree, that the most radical Christian claim of all is to say we are a family. Yet it is the absolute foundation of our faith. Like my friend and his son, like the people of our Gospel lesson, like the priest and the people of his village, we can be as different as night and day. And yet, we can discover that we are all bound on the same journey, with the same hopes, fears, and dreams. Not that this is ever easy. It can be hard to live as a family. It can be hard to forgive; it can be hard to listen; it can be hard to heal; it can be hard to love. We can be sure that living as a family will upset the status quo. But in the end, this miracle of family is more spectacular than any other.

It didn't take me long to learn this after graduating from seminary. I had been on the job for only a couple weeks when I caught several children playing in the parish hall of Saint John's in Montgomery. These were not children of parishioners, mind you; these were neighborhood children, children from one of the poorest and most dangerous housing communities in town. Still, they seemed quite at home, since they had been to Saint John's the year before for Bible school. I told them gently that they couldn't run around in the parish hall (an admonishment usually reserved for my own children), but that they were always welcome to return when the church was open. "When's that?" they asked immediately. I was taken aback. "Uh . . . well, on Sundays we are open," I managed to stammer, certain I would never see them again.

The next day, which was Sunday, our church sexton walked up to me and complained, "Those kids you invited to church are in the kitchen having breakfast, and they sure do eat a lot!" As it turned out, they stayed all morning. After breakfast, they went to church, and after that, they attended the main service, sitting with a woman they already knew as "Miz Young" from their school. When it came time for communion, "Miz Young" brought them up to the altar rail. She coached them well, as their arms were already folded and ready for a blessing from the priest. The only problem with her plan was that I was serving on their side of the altar rail that day, and being a newly ordained deacon, I was not permitted to do "priest stuff," such as blessings. Still, I wanted their trip to the altar to be special, so I did something I had seen other clergy do, though I suspect I was not really authorized. I traced a cross on each child's forehead. After church, "Miz Young" told me the crosses were a hit. "What did that man put on my head, Miz Young? Can you see that cross? Will it wash off?" She answered their questions with patience and wisdom, telling them that the cross was to remind them that they belong to God, and that while it will never wash off, their sins had been washed away. One little boy promptly and joyfully replied, "Well, I will go and sin no more!"

That next week, I was in the office with my boss when a little head popped around the corner. It was one of the children from Sunday, and he had a child in tow I hadn't seen before. "Excuse me," he said, "but Chili here needs to see the preacher." Assuming he meant me, I asked, "Well, what does Chili want?" He answered, "Chili needs to get one of them crosses." We prayed quietly in my office, and it occurred to me that seminaries are nice, ordination certificates are nice, bishops are nice, but it's people like Chili who ordain us as disciples of the Lord. I like to say my ordained ministry began that day.

Which brings us back to our scene from Cronin's novel. Shortly before leaving China for his native Scotland, the retiring priest received a last visit from his old friend. The merchant was the wealthiest man in the village, and their relationship had been forged years before, when Chisholm cared for his sick child. On this day, he simply wanted to know whether he would ever see the priest again. "Never," Chisholm replied. "We must look forward to our meeting in the celestial hereafter."

In polite Chinese society, it was not common or encouraged to ever be direct in a conversation, but this time, the friend minced no words. "My dear Father Chisholm," he began, "I have often said that there are many religions, and each has its gate to heaven. Now it would appear that I have the extraordinary desire to enter by your gate." The old priest was dumbfounded. He had rarely converted anyone, yet standing before him was a man—the most powerful man in town—joining him as a follower of Jesus Christ. "You can't be serious," Chisholm replied.

But the Chinese gentleman was determined. He saw something that was generally lost on the crowds begging at the mission door. He saw something in the life of the old priest that had changed his own life forever. It was the miracle of family. "Many years ago, when you cured my son, I was not serious. But then I was unaware of the nature of your life . . . of its patience, quietness, and courage. The goodness of a religion is best judged by the goodness of its adherents. My friend, you have conquered me by example."

Sisters and Brothers, the world is starving for the Gospel we carry in our hearts. We long to be whole; we long to be free; we long to know that we are not alone. We long for family. May God give us the courage and the will to share this Good News wherever we go, to fearlessly conquer with love, and to spread God's Kingdom throughout the world.

NOTE

1. A. J. Cronin, *The Keys of the Kingdom* (Boston: Little, Brown & Co., 1941), 255–56.

CHAPTER 7

LOVE ONE ANOTHER

A snapshot for the end of a journey

When he had gone out, Jesus said, "Now the Son of Man has been glorified, and God has been glorified in him. If God has been glorified in him, God will also glorify him in himself and will glorify him at once. Little children, I am with you only a little longer. You will look for me; and as I said to the Jews so now I say to you, 'Where I am going, you cannot come.' I give you a new commandment, that you love one another. Just as I have loved you, you should also love one another. By this everyone will know that

*you are my disciples, if you have love for one
another."*

John 13:31–35

A Kentucky author and preacher named Paul Prather tells the
story of a little church that died one day, and of seven women
who got the surprise of their lives.[1] Johnson Branch Baptist
Church sat on the same plot of land for more than a hundred
years, and it was the scene of countless revivals, bake sales, bap-
tisms, and potluck suppers. It was built to hold more than two
hundred souls, and old-timers could still remember the days
when folding chairs lined the walls for a spillover crowd and
Sunday school classes were filled to capacity. But that was just a
memory now, and a distant one at that. One could point to several reasons for the decline. With the new bypass completed just
west of town, traffic patterns had changed along Johnson Branch
Road, as had the demographics of the congregation. Children
grew up and moved away, parents grew old and died, until all
that remained were seven old women, scattered across the empty
pews on a Sunday morning.

On this particular morning, the faithful remnant gathered in
the sanctuary—along with assorted canes and walkers—for a
final service of worship. The local Baptist Association had long
stopped sending ministers to serve the tiny congregation, so the
preacher that morning was a student from the local Bible college.
One of the women played hymns on an old, untuned piano,
while another passed the plate around for the last collection.

To be honest, I can relate to this scene, as it reminds me of a journey I recently took. I was driving from Decatur to a funeral in Tuscaloosa, when I decided on a whim to take the Downtown Bessemer exit off I-59. I simply wanted a quick look at the church of my childhood; my parents had moved from Bessemer almost twenty years ago, and it had been even longer since I had seen First Baptist. Much about the place had changed. The town has gone through a revival of sorts, with outlet shopping and a theme park nearby, but it was evident that my old church had fallen on hard times. The building needed a coat of paint, and tall weeds choked the flower beds out front. Cracked windows, potholes, even graffiti on the back wall spoke of a congregation on its last legs. It seemed to me that if my old church hadn't died, it was at best, to borrow T. S. Eliot's phrase, "partly living." Tough-looking characters loitered nearby, and these kept me from staying too long in the parking lot—a place where I had spent hours playing with my friends, a place where I had learned about cars and girls, a place where I had waited under warm starlight for my folks to finish with choir practice. Even that parking lot had been sacred once, but it was just a memory now.

Of all the snapshots we might find for comfort at the end of such journeys, I can't think of a better picture than the one we find in the thirteenth chapter of John's Gospel. After all, it is here that we read of Jesus sharing a last meal with his friends. They, too, are approaching the end of a long journey together, and they all know it. One of their own has slipped into the night to betray Jesus, and in a few short hours, their world will be coming to an end. This scene, like the church of my childhood or the one on Johnson Branch Road, stands to remind us that life doesn't always work out as we hoped or planned. If we are honest about it, even the best of journeys come to an end. But God continues, and his grace is more than we can ask or imagine.

It has been said that we live in a culture that so values the freedom to choose that we tend to forget that, more often than not, life chooses us.[2] This makes sense if we think about it. Loved ones die, jobs change or end, people hurt us, accidents happen, and all too often we are left to face an uncertain future. Our Gospel doesn't promise that bad things will never happen or that journeys will never end. Still, we have hope because we never journey alone. All through the changes and chances of our lives there remains a constant—the abiding love of God, in us and among us always. If we only try, we can all look back and see the hand of God at work, protecting, guiding, healing, consoling, calling us home.

Every so often I treat myself and take home communion out to church members. I call it a treat because taking a communion kit—a box filled with bread, wine, and a tiny chalice—to people who want the sacrament but can't make it to church is one of my favorite things to do. This in itself is an interesting fact, as home communions used to scare me to death. For starters, though it might be called "home communion," it rarely happens in a home. Rather, this service is usually conducted in places not at all suited for prayer—hospital rooms, nursing home rooms, and the like. These are places where orderlies wander in during the

Lord's Prayer, where intercoms buzz, where it is entirely possible to barge in on someone's sponge bath. Add to all these distractions the fact that one must juggle a prayer book and tiny tea set of communion vessels, and you get the picture. As a seminarian, I once took communion to a woman in the hospital, and since we were in a tiny semiprivate room, I sat on the edge of her bed. Now I thought this to be a cozy arrangement, until she started mumbling something softly (a prayer perhaps?). I leaned closer, and she said to me, "Get off my oxygen tube, boy. I can't breathe."

It took a little time, but it slowly began to dawn on me that the distractions and awkwardness of it all were really okay. I was learning something of the presence of God, even in the mess, even when life doesn't seem to work out as we had hoped or planned, even in the midst of pain and uncertainty, even at the end of our journeys. After all, since God is especially present when we go to a little extra trouble for another, so what if there is no place to sit? For a time, I had the great pleasure of driving to a north Alabama nursing home every other week with a man we called Judge Bibb. He rode with me (I wouldn't let him drive, though he offered every time) to see his wife, Jean, to share communion together. It was always the same. I would place the bread and wine on a bedside table, and we would say our prayers. Then the old judge would sing to his bride of fifty-seven years a hymn they knew from church: "Bread of the world in mercy broken, Wine of the soul in mercy shed . . ." God was present, especially present, and in that room I was not only given a glimpse of true love between two old people, but also reminded that even a wheelchair can be a front-row seat to the Holy of Holies.

This scene seems to me to come right out of the Gospel of John. After all, as Jesus and his friends sat around the table for the last time, he reminded them to love one another as he had loved them all along. They couldn't fully know what was in store for them as they broke bread with the Lord. It would be a dark and scary time before they could see that on the other side of death, there is always resurrection. But even in the midst of uncertainty, they had each other, and this would be enough. They could love one another and feel the presence of God in their midst. They could be so good to one another that they, too, would remind a hurting and broken world of the Good News of Jesus—which reminds me to finish telling you the story of the last Sunday at the church on Johnson Branch Road.

After the service was finally over, the seven women ambled into the fellowship hall, where they would dine on a last meal of potato salad and deviled eggs. As they gathered around the table, one of them stood up. "Ladies," she began, "I have been asking the Lord for the right time to do this. Y'all might recall that I took the church records back to my apartment some weeks ago, and when I sat down to balance the checkbook, I found that the church still had $900 in the account." Their eyes grew wide as she pulled out a wad of white envelopes from her purse. "Therefore, I have enough in the account to pay the preacher today and to keep the grass mowed till fall. The rest is yours. You get $100 apiece as a 'going-away present.'"

The women were silent and teary. Without exception, they were on fixed incomes, and one of them had had to do without her blood thinner the month before. They tore into their envelopes and took out their crisp, new bills. One of them rolled hers into a cigar, saying between fake puffs, "I always did think I would make a good tycoon." All of them giggled like schoolgirls for the rest of the afternoon.

Journeys will end. Circumstances will change. Life may turn out very different than we ever expected. But new adventures await us. God is with us, always with us, leading us all into the mystery of love.

NOTES

1. Paul Prather, "The Faithful," *Lousville Review*, 2002. Reprinted in Shannon Ravenel, ed., *New Stories from the South, 2003* (Chapel Hill, NC: Algonquin Books of Chapel Hill, 2003), 199–215.

2. Barbara Brown Taylor, *Gospel Medicine* (Boston: Cowley Publications, 1995), 152.

CHAPTER 8

LIFE IS GOOD

A snapshot for rule followers

Now before faith came, we were imprisoned and guarded under the law until faith would be revealed. Therefore the law was our disciplinarian until Christ came, so that we might be justified by faith. But now that faith has come, we are no longer subject to a disciplinarian, for in Christ Jesus you are children of God through faith.

Galatians 3:23–26

In a fictional short story titled "Behold," Tim Melley tells of the day a little boy discovered that life is good, though it happened on what was probably the most depressing day of the year for him.[1] It happened on Good Friday, a day when the little boy and his family spent most of the afternoon in the darkened nave of Saint Agatha's church. "For a Catholic kid in those days," Melley writes, "there was nothing good about Good Friday. From dawn to dusk we had to fast on toast and tea, and when we were good and starving we had to choke down a bowl of Mom's fish stew." This year was especially hard, since his mom wasn't even with them. She had been battling cancer for almost a year and didn't have the stamina to make it through the entire service.

He was serving as an altar boy on this day, and while the lector read from the Passion Gospel, he noticed his mother walking slowly down the aisle and sitting stiffly with his brothers and sisters. As his father helped her into the pew, the boy wondered why God acted the way he did. After all, the little boy had been praying for a year for God to heal his mother; he went to mass every week; he never missed a confession. He knew the rules and he kept them all. Still his mother suffered.

After the lector was finished, then came the boy's cue to pick up the wooden cross leaning against the altar and follow the priest into the congregation. He was a good acolyte, a real veteran, but since it was Good Friday, he was also dizzy with hunger, which is the only plausible explanation for what happened next. He stopped midway down the aisle, just as instructed, and held the cross high as the priest began to sing, "Behold, the wood of the cross, on which hung the savior of the world." Then disaster struck. The little boy started to laugh. He couldn't help it—the priest was supposed to be singing, but to the boy, he sounded more like a baby seal being slaughtered. Little flecks of spit flew everywhere, and as the priest bellowed, the altar boy could see the silver molars in the back of the man's mouth. It was hysterical.

Of course, he tried not to laugh, but he couldn't help himself. He stared at the carpet; he tried to think of himself being tortured; he avoided the gaze of his classmates—all smiling and ribbing each other at the sight of an altar boy beginning to crack. He even closed his eyes, but he couldn't help it. The priest bellowed again, and another snort huffed out of his nose. By this time, the congregation was laughing as well. Well, most of the congregation was laughing. The boy's father stared with a look that suggested his son had just committed murder, and he motioned for the boy to "cut it out."

I can certainly relate to this story, since I have an acolyte of my own at home. A couple years ago during Sunday announcements in church, my son, Copeland, gave me a surprise I will never forget. Going through the calendar of events that day, I reminded the congregation of an ice-skating trip scheduled for the teenagers, when Copeland, who was ten years old and serving as an acolyte that day, suddenly raised his hand to ask a question. Needless to say, I wasn't prepared for this distraction. Announcements are among my least favorite things to do on a Sunday morning, if only because I get nervous and sometimes forget to mention an important luncheon or remind people to fill out their visitors' cards. Adding to my stress this day was the fact that it was Copeland who was asking the question in front of all those people, and there was just no telling what he might say.

I looked at my son sweetly, knowing that hundreds of eyes were watching this unexpected interchange between father and son. "Just a minute," I told him as I finished my announcements for the day, complete with a birthday prayer and a welcome to newcomers. Copeland's hand remained raised throughout. I was sweating; the congregation was giggling. Finally I was finished, so I looked at my boy and asked, "Yes, son, how can I help you?" His eyes narrowed; he didn't crack a smile. He simply said, "How come you never take me skating?" I hissed, "*Be quiet, Copeland,*" before turning to the congregation with open arms and saying, "Walk in love as Christ loved us . . ."

Of course, later we went skating.

For the little boy in church that Good Friday, the hysterical feeling suddenly slipped away. This was a serious breach of the rules, and he knew it. The laughing acolyte had just disgraced his mother on the most serious day of the year. And yet, as he risked a glance in her direction, he could see her doubled over and shaking. She was not crying or shaking with anger. She was laughing.

He knew that laugh. That was her belly laugh, her vacation at Cape Cod laugh, her playing with the kids in the backyard laugh, her "life is good, life is good, life is good" laugh. It was here, on the most depressing day of the year, that a little boy discovered the joy of living. It was here, even as he failed to follow the rules, that he discovered that God loves his children. It was here, underneath the pain, underneath the failure, underneath the disappointment, the regret, the uncertainty, even the tears, that he discovered that *life is good*.

Now it occurs to me that Saint Paul had pretty much the same thing in mind when he wrote his letter to the Galatians. Of all the snapshots we find in the New Testament, I have often wondered how this one got in the scrapbook. If the letters of Paul are indeed correspondence between a particular church community and their former pastor, then I am sorry for the Galatians that we get to read this particular piece of mail. Unlike the other letters of Paul, where he is glowing in his praise and encourages the churches to carry on the work, in this one he gets right down to business. Paul is disappointed, and the reason is simple enough. The church had gotten off to a pretty good start in that part of the world, but at some point, the Christians in Galatia forgot that life is good. In other words, they were so busy trying to earn their spots in heaven that they forgot what Paul had told them from the very beginning—that by the power of Christ, not by their rules, their spots had already been won for them. They simply forgot they were free—free from the rules that demand grudging obedience, free from the worry that they had done enough, free to live as God's children, free to laugh, free to love, free to live.

Of course, we shouldn't be too hard on the Galatians. It is easy to forget that life is good. Sometimes I think we are prisoners of our own low expectations. We tell ourselves we know what is possible, what is not possible. We set up rules for ourselves, and we follow them so well. We work at our jobs, we raise our families, we pay our taxes, we coach Little League. If we are really good people, then we come to church, we serve on committees, we teach Bible school. But mostly we just hang on and hope for the best.

And when the heart attack happens, when the friends are divorced, when the children are distant, when the business fails, when loved ones hurt us, we simply hang our heads and wonder if we've done enough. But the Good News of the Gospel is simply this: God in Christ holds out a new life for each of us that is always more than we can ask or imagine or gain on our own. God in Christ wants us to accept this new life right now, to *live* this new life right now—where every day is an adventure, every job is a calling, every neighbor is a beloved brother and sister, every day is a gift.

Let me see if I can say it another way. Each night before we put our children to bed, we say our family prayers together. Being southern children, their prayers always include the same refrain during the winter months: "Please Lord, let it snow." I don't join them. That's the difference between a child and someone with grown-up responsibilities. They are thinking sleds and a day off from school; I am thinking icy roads and long lines at the grocery store, where all they have is skim milk. To be honest, I haven't prayed for snow since the blizzard of 1996. We were in seminary back then, and the entire eastern seaboard was covered in a blanket of snow and ice. But that's not what I remember. I remember being trapped in an apartment for four days, in a tiny apartment with my children, who were then ages two and four. It was an experience of togetherness I will never forget.

Maybe it was cabin fever, but all the rules of the house went straight out the window: "Betsy, don't mix your applesauce with ketchup; that's gross!" "No, Copeland, you may not wear a ski mask to the table, and you may not wear a football helmet to bed." "Don't you children want to watch another video? That's the tenth time you've watched Barney this morning." "What difference does it make whether your milk is in a blue cup or a red cup?" It took me a while to learn this, but I did eventually figure out that things that seemed utter foolishness to me made perfect sense to them. Hey, it's okay to mix your two favorite foods (applesauce and ketchup), since you can always play with it if doesn't taste so good. A ski mask is not acceptable at the dinner table, unless, of course, you are Spider-Man and the safety of the free world depends on your disguise. There is nothing *really* wrong with watching a video ten times in a row, and maybe milk does taste better in a blue cup. No, what seemed like foolishness to me was in fact imagination hard at work, where a football helmet becomes an astronaut's life-support system or a bread basket becomes a catcher's mask. With my own adult sense and sensibility, I was trapped in a tiny apartment. But my children were free to travel all over creation.

Please don't misunderstand. I'm not saying that rules are unimportant. Rules guide, rules protect, rules help us discover who we are as children of God. But I am asking us to remember what Paul told the church in Galatia that day. Don't forget to look for the surprise. Life is God's gift to us, and there is just no telling what can happen when we discover the joy of living. Remember, life is good.

NOTE

1. Tim Melley, "Behold," *The Sun* 342 (June 2004).

CHAPTER 9

A TOWN WHERE
MAGIC HAPPENED

A snapshot of the Kingdom of God

> *Then he looked up at his disciples and said,*
> *"Blessed are you who are poor, for yours is the*
> *kingdom of God."*
>
> Luke 6:20

A *Sports Illustrated* writer named Gary Smith wrote a story a few years ago about a little town where magic happened.[1] It was a magic that began the day they hired a new basketball coach, a magic that changed the town of Berlin, Ohio, forever.

To understand this story, you first need to know that Berlin, Ohio, lies in the heart of Amish and Mennonite country. Berlin is a town without high school football, without a traffic light, without a fast-food restaurant. There is only basketball, Hiland High basketball, and the new coach wasn't just any man—he was a black man, the only black man in the county. He was also single, in a town where marriage and children were expected of pretty much everyone, and he was Roman Catholic, in a place where children grew up with tales of persecution by Catholics in the Old Country.

Needless to say, people weren't exactly thrilled with the new choice for head coach. In this closed community, it was as if their world had been turned upside down. In no time at all, complaints were filed with the school board, racial slurs were muttered in the local diner, and as Coach walked down the street, the locals gave him a wide berth. But winning changed all that. As Gary Smith writes, "In no time at all, Coach had a team of spindly, short Mennonite kids runnin' and gunnin', chucking up threes and full court pressing from buzzer to buzzer." In no time at all, the Hiland High gym became a madhouse on Friday nights—the only place where a Mennonite farmer could scream his head off, a place where fans were packed from wall to wall. Why, even the local Amish were into the game, hitching their buggies across the street from the gym or secretly catching the game on WKLM from a radio hidden inside the barn.

The winning continued year after year, and Coach never let the school down. His players worshiped him, and boys who had never dreamed of life beyond their fathers' lumbermill began to go to college. Naturally, Coach caught the attention of bigger athletic programs, and scouts came down from big cities like Canton and Akron. But Coach wasn't interested in more money or prestige. Something deeper kept him in Berlin, something deeper even than winning, and though he could have named his price, Coach stayed.

It was magic all right, but still not the magic they talk about these days. The real magic happened over time, the real magic sneaked in, while the town was celebrating eleven conference titles and five semifinals. The real magic happened when a town who had never even seen a black man before welcomed him into their homes, and into their arms. The real magic happened when a Roman Catholic managed to find himself deeply loved by people raised on fear of Roman Catholics. The real magic happened when long-held opinions and prejudices were forgotten, and a little town discovered a world they never dreamed of before.

I think there is a lesson here akin to the snapshot we find in the sixth chapter of Luke. To begin with, this verse, like the story of Berlin, Ohio, tells of a stunning reversal. In other words, I don't believe that crowds followed Jesus in the early days of his ministry just because they wanted to see a miracle. True, there was no telling what you might see in those days. But I believe that crowds followed Jesus everywhere simply because no one ever heard anyone like him before. Here in the sixth chapter, one can almost hear them muttering among themselves as Jesus turned their world upside down. "Blessed are the poor," he told them in effect, "for yours is the kingdom of God. Blessed are the hungry, blessed are the brokenhearted, blessed are the hated, blessed are the forgotten, blessed are the voiceless, blessed are the different, blessed are those you might never expect to be loved and valued by God." And as if this wasn't enough, he added, "But woe to you who are rich, for you have received your consolation." Which was Jesus' way of saying that those who are smug or satisfied, those who hang on to their opinions or prejudices, those who assume they are more special than others, those who are immune to suffering, those who are merely content to leave the world as it is are likely to miss out on the magic.

I keep a little prayer in my office called a "Christmas Prayer." It came inside a Christmas card a while back, and I thought it was really profound—especially since it didn't say anything about Christmas. Rather, it gives just a glimpse of life as it is meant to be lived, and maybe even a way to allow the magic to enter our own lives. Some of the prayer goes like this:

"Heavenly Father, help us to remember that the jerk who cut us off in traffic last night is in fact a single mother who worked nine hours that day, who was rushing home to cook dinner, to help her children with their homework, to do the laundry, and spend precious moments with her family.

"Help us to remember that the pierced and tattooed young man who can't make change at the convenience store is in fact a worried college student, balancing his apprehension over final exams with his fear of not getting student loans for the next semester.

"Remind us that the scary looking bum, begging for money day after day in the same spot, is in fact slave to addictions we can only imagine in our worst nightmares."

Please don't misunderstand. I don't believe this snapshot means that God likes another group of people better than us, and I don't think it is a call to be nice simply because Jesus was nice. Rather, I believe it is a call to see the world as God sees the world, a reminder that God loves all of his children—with a love that heals all our wounds, hears all our cries, wipes every tear from our eyes. Which leaves us with a challenge: In the face of such love, what else can we do but give back?

Let me see if I can put this some other way. Some years ago, I was given the task of recruiting teachers for sixth-grade Sunday school. I asked a friend if he would help, and his answer surprised me. "Rich, I'll teach the class," he said, then added gravely, "but only because I want to go to heaven someday." I had to think about that for a moment. I told him that if anything would get you into heaven, it would have to be teaching sixth-grade Sunday school. But God doesn't work that way. We come to church, we love our neighbor, we forgive those who hurt us, we do the work, we say our prayers—not because we hope to be saved, but because we have been saved. That said, when we know deep down that God loves us this much, then it's really not enough to share that love merely with those who are closest to us, or those who look like us, or think like us, or act like us. If we only try, if we only pay attention, if we only open our hearts, then we, too, can discover God's love in the most surprising places. We can enter a world we never imagined. We can live in a world where magic happens.

When Coach died in the early 1990s, the town of Berlin, Ohio, was devastated. Grown men wept. One of the players quit going to church for months, until he figured it was silly to claim there was no God when he had been looking at a miracle all his life. Tattoo parlors added Mennonites to their clientele, as young men started putting Coach's name on their arms. A scholarship fund was created, and donations started pouring in. But a deeper magic was at work here, deeper than the memory of a good man and a winning coach. Coach's life had become a moral compass for this deeply moral community. One former player decided he would reverse Coach's path and coach inner-city kids. Couples in the county began to adopt black children and Latino children from the bigger cities. People around town began asking themselves when confronted with a moral dilemma: "What would Coach do?"

The funeral was held at Saint Peter's Catholic Church in Millersburg. The church was packed that day, and as the priest looked out over the congregation, he could hardly believe what he saw. Mennonites from Berlin in their white veils and simple clothing, Coach's Baptist cousins from Columbus, and the Catholic faithful of Millersburg all sat together—thanking God for the life of the man they loved. And though he knew it wasn't allowed, though he knew it could get him into trouble, the priest did something he knew Coach would do: He invited everyone up to receive communion. The congregation knew

Coach, too, so they rose at the invitation and poured toward the altar. It was magic all right, and this magic has a name. We call it the Kingdom of God.

NOTE

1. Gary Smith, "Higher Education," *Sports Illustrated*, March 5, 2001. Reprinted in Dave Eggers, ed., *The Best American Nonrequired Reading, 2002* (Boston and New York: Houghton Mifflin Co., 2002), 193–215.

CHAPTER 10

SALVATION

*A snapshot to remind us
we are never alone*

*Just after daybreak, Jesus stood on the beach; but
the disciples did not know it was Jesus. Jesus said
to them, "Children, you have no fish, have you?"
They answered him, "No." He said to them,
"Cast the net to the right side and you will find
some." So they cast it, and now they were not able
to haul it in because there were so many fish.
That disciple whom Jesus loved said to Peter, "It
is the Lord!" When Simon Peter heard that it was
the Lord, he put on some clothes, for he was
naked, and jumped into the sea.*

John 21: 4–7

I ran across a little story a few years ago that I don't think I will ever forget.[1] It's a simple story, really, a story about salvation, and it all began the day a young mother got a disconnect notice in the mail. This was a new experience for her, and it was pretty scary. She was raised in a financially secure family; she grew up learning to pay her bills. Still, her divorce had put her behind, and her son's illness put her far behind. For weeks, the bills had been mounting, and now her phone was going to be cut off. Burdened by shame and consumed with worry, she seemed caught in a hopeless situation; she felt so alone. But just as she was wondering what to do next, she heard something on the radio that seemed to be her salvation. A news report announced that the price of gold was at an all-time high—over $200 an ounce. Immediately, she went to the bedroom and found the little box she kept in the back of the dresser drawer, containing a wedding band, a high school ring, and a ring with her grandmother's initials etched on the side. Together, these had to be more than three ounces. Together, they had to cover the bills.

It was raining hard when she loaded her eight-year-old and the two toddlers in the car, but she knew this was a journey that couldn't wait. As she drove into town, it didn't take long for her to find what she was looking for—a metal building with a sign out front: "Pawn Shop. Get Rich Quick." She parked where she could see her kids in the car, and then hurried through the heavy front door. The dim room was filled with other people's treasures: VCRs, saxophones, crescent wrench sets. As she handed her box to the man behind the counter, hope welled up in her heart. It didn't take him long to answer: "Not much here. I'll give you thirty-five bucks for all three." The young mother stared in disbelief. She couldn't believe what she just heard. "But what about the price of gold?" she asked. The man laughed; a customer in the back laughed as well. "That don't mean nothing to me, lady," he replied. "Take it or leave it."

She picked up her little box and turned away, devastated. And just as it seemed that her world was collapsing around her, she saw. The rain had stopped and the sun had come out, shining like gold on the faces of her children. These were her treasures, after all, and their eyes danced with innocence and joy. She was not alone; they were not alone. The clouds were parted, and together they could all face the future in hope. "Are we rich, Mama?" her eight-year-old asked with a giggle. "You bet we are," she said. "Let's go get some ice cream." And they did.

This may not seem at first to be a story about salvation. On the one hand, we don't really know what the future would hold for this young family, or how the woman would pay her bills in the end. On the other hand, we usually think of salvation as a "churchy" word that indicates something that happens to us when we die—streets of gold, mansions in the sky, and all that. This is what people usually mean when they ask us if we are "saved." But there is another meaning to the word, another understanding of salvation that has as much to do with the here and now as it does with the hope of heaven. In other words, salvation can happen when we discover we are not alone and we look to the future in hope. Salvation can happen when we figure out that our lives do matter, our choices do matter, and we have a place in God's universe. Salvation can happen when we know that we are watched over, cared for, somehow more *alive* than ever before.

I believe something akin to salvation happened in that pawn shop parking lot, just as it happened on the beach beside the sea of Tiberias.

I've long wondered why the Gospel of John would end with such a simple, quiet little snapshot. Peter, it seems, had gone back to his old job of fishing and had taken his friends along with him. Of course, things were not the same as before—they couldn't be, since Jesus had been raised from the dead. They had seen him in the flesh and had even seen the scars.

Still, Jesus wasn't with them in the boat that night, and we aren't told what they were thinking as they cast their nets in vain. We also don't know what they were thinking at daybreak, when that familiar voice called out over the waves. Our Bible translates the word as "children," but the original word was closer to "lads," for they were Jesus' pals, after all, and standing on the shore, he suggested they try their hand at fishing just one more time. When they began to haul in the fish, *they saw*. They were not alone, after all.

Peter was so excited that he jumped right out of the boat, but what followed was nothing particularly miraculous; just a meal of bread and fish shared with their old friend. And that's pretty much it. John's Gospel ends a few verses later, right on the beach.

And yet, there is more to this story than meets the eye. We may scratch our heads in wonder over the simplicity of it all, but the more we consider how God works in our own lives, the more this story makes sense—for Peter and for us.

I'll be the first to admit that I long for signs from God. I am always on the hunt for some proof of God's existence—something irrefutable, something dramatic, something to settle any doubt once and for all. Recently, I read the transcript of an interview conducted in the 1930s as part of the Federal Writers' Project, wherein writers were given the task of recording the narratives of people who had a living memory of slavery in the United States.[2] The interview was with an old black gentleman from Florence, Alabama, who claimed to be 112 and remembered the meteor shower of 1833, now known as the "stars that fell on Alabama." He was just a little boy when it happened; his family hid inside the cabin, expecting the world to come to an end. But the old man still remembered the day, when he stayed outside and saw streaks of light "falling from the sky like pitch dropping off a pine torch."

That's the kind of sign I want: something splashed across the sky. But I also know that to be really honest about it, signs like these still wouldn't reach the depths of my soul. After all, it is not enough to know that God is way up in the sky somewhere. Rather, what I long for is to know that the same God who set the planets in their courses also knows my name. I long to know that God is more than present among the stars, but also present in the daily business of my life. I long to know that God laughs when I laugh, cries when I cry. I long to know that I am watched over and cared for, in this world and the next.

Speaking of that, I have my own simple story to hang on to these days. Every week, my office routine is fairly set. Thursday is my day for sermon writing, period. When this is not practical, I can usually arrange things to get something done for Sunday. One week, however, I was really stuck. My week was chock-full of appointments, and on Thursday I was called in for an emergency visit to a hospital in a neighboring city. Of course, I was happy to go; in fact, I needed to go, but even the weekend was full. When would I write a sermon for Sunday? Needless to say, I began to worry as I drove down the highway.

As I walked into the lobby of the hospital, I saw it. The very Gospel lesson appointed for Sunday was emblazoned on the wall. Coincidence? Perhaps, but I don't think so. I believe God was reminding me in that very instant of the meaning of salvation. That is, God is very near to us; our job is to listen, watch, and trust. God is the giver of sermons, after all. God is the giver of life, love, and peace, and everything else we might long for. And though it is hard to explain or describe, I walked into that hospital feeling relieved, much like the young mother in the parking lot that day. I had everything I needed.

This is the news that had Peter jumping right out of that boat. God is with us, every day. This is our Gospel, and when we discover the treasure we truly long for, then we, too, can experience salvation. To be fair, I suppose you could ask for a little more proof that all of this is true. These are quiet little stories, after all.

But ours is a Gospel that isn't written in the stars. It is written in our lives, and I can tell you why I believe. I believe because of all the times in my life that I felt God beside me—in times of joy, especially in times of sorrow and desperation, and from time to time in those quiet ordinary moments I can define only as peace.

I have made mistakes; I certainly have my share of regrets. There have been times when it seems the whole world has collapsed around me. But there have also been those times when the clouds parted, reminding me that God is very near. This snapshot, like these stories, remind me that God has been there all along—through so much in my everyday life that I know deep down God will be with me beyond the grave as well. Guess what? God knows you, too.

Are we rich? You bet we are.

NOTES

1. Pat Gibson Owen, "Reader Write: Debt," *The Sun* 310 (October 2001), 37.

2. Horace Randall Williams, *Weren't No Good Times* (Winston-Salem, NC: John F. Blair, 2004), 70.

CHAPTER 11

LOST AND FOUND

A snapshot of unending hope

So Jesus told them this parable: "Which one of you, having a hundred sheep and losing one of them, does not leave the ninety nine in the wilderness and go after the one that is lost until he finds it? When he has found it, he lays it on his shoulders and rejoices."

Luke 15:3–5

"Or what woman having ten silver coins, if she loses one of them, does not light a lamp, sweep the house, and search carefully until she finds it?

When she has found it, she calls together her
friends and neighbors, saying, 'Rejoice with me,
for I have found the coin that I had lost.'"

Luke 15:8–9

I used to read to my children before bedtime. Before they were old enough to do their own reading, it was one of our favorite things to do as a family. If you were to ask the kids to name the book they enjoyed the most with Daddy, both would tell you it was *To Kill a Mockingbird*, by Harper Lee. It is my favorite book, and it was my idea to read it, though I knew there would be some risk. After all, there are some pretty adult themes in this book: namely, the trial of a black man wrongfully accused of assaulting a white woman in Depression-era Alabama, and the struggles of a lawyer named Atticus Finch, who aimed to defend him. But I also knew that the children would be thrilled with the adventures of Atticus's children, Jem and Scout, who, along with their friend Dill, spent long summers scheming to make the spectral Boo Radley come out of his house.

I think what made this the most fun for the children was the fact that I read the book like an old cliffhanger movie, leaving them to wonder what would happen next. Would Mrs. Dubose punish Jem for destroying her camellias? Would Miss Maudie rebuild her house after the fire? Would Scout finish the school year without a fight? We would have to wait and see.

When we got closer to the trial itself, I was careful to explain to my beautiful, color-blind children how people can fear and hate one another just because they are different somehow. I told them about growing up during the last days of segregation and asking my mother one day why one public restroom said, "White," and another said, "Colored." I told them that fear and hatred made the trial very dangerous for the black man, and for Atticus. My children were on the edge of their seats as I read the account of the trial and of Atticus punching holes in the shaky case put forth by the prosecution. The defendant, Tom Robinson, was clearly an innocent man, and I tried to sound as much like Gregory Peck as I possibly could as I read of Atticus standing before the jurors and saying, "For God's sake do your duty."

Betsy clapped. This was the best cliffhanger of all. "Hooray for Atticus," she cheered, and when I asked her why she was so happy, she said it was because tomorrow night she would learn how Atticus won the trial, and Tom Robinson would go home to his wife and family. My heart sank.

My heart sank because I didn't have to wait and see. My heart sank because I already knew how the story went. My heart sank because I knew the jurors would not do their duty that day. My heart sank because I knew that fear and hatred would conspire to condemn an innocent man. My heart sank because I knew that Betsy would have to learn that good guys don't always win, that justice isn't always served, that stories don't always have happy endings. This is why Boo Radley wouldn't come out of his house, after all. My heart sank because I knew Betsy would lose her innocence—right before bedtime.

As much as we try to keep it from our children, loss of innocence is just a part of life. It has been said that loss itself is a part
of life, whether we are talking about lost innocence, or love, or
heart, or hope; at some point, we will lose something or someone
dear to us. We lose our loved ones though separation, divorce,
death. We lose our youthful vigor; we lose memories we thought
we would never forget. Sometimes we lose our health, and eventually we lose our lives. No one escapes. And yet, loss doesn't
have the last word in our story, or at least it doesn't have to. The
Good News of our Gospel could be summed up in this way:
What may be lost to us is never lost to God. We lose, but God
saves. I think this lies at the very heart of Jesus' stories about the
sheep and the coin. The picture of the little lost sheep reminds
us that we are infinitely valuable to God, no matter where we go;
no matter what we have done. The coin reminds us that our own
hopes and dreams and loves are valuable to God as well.[1]

Everyone who knows me knows that I just love a good idea,
and I am willing to try just about anything once if I get excited
about it. I am famous in Montgomery for one of these big ideas,
and though it wasn't exactly a disaster, I'll probably never try it
again. The idea was to reenact the parable of the lost sheep by
bringing a little lamb to Vacation Bible School. A friend of mine
brought the lamb from his farm; the plan was for the little fellow
to frolic and play inside the playground fence while classes of
children could file by and pet him.

It seemed like the perfect setup at first. The lamb nibbled grass
while the clergy and a few teachers sipped coffee and waited for

the children. Suddenly, however, the lamb slipped through the bars of the fence and ran out into the busy street alongside the church. This was a problem. We were all inside the fence; the lamb was outside. In no time at all, we heard screeching tires and honking horns as cars swerved to avoid the terrified animal.

At the moment, there seemed to be only two ways to solve the problem. Our rector chose to climb the fence in his suit (forgetting that a sixth-grader had broken his arm doing that very thing), while my friend and I ran back through the parish hall and to the street. Later, I asked our parish cook why she didn't help when, from the kitchen, she saw us running through the parish hall. She confessed that when she heard there was a lamb in the middle of Jefferson Street, she started looking for the mint jelly. At any rate, my friend got to the lamb first, and I am glad he did, since he knew more about this sort of thing than I did. In order to catch the lamb, he had to throw himself on top of the creature and hold it, mewling and kicking and screaming, against his chest.

Our plan changed after that. There would be no frolicking in the grass. My friend brought our little lost lamb into the church, still kicking but now safe. As luck would have it, he walked into the church under a window depicting Christ holding a little lamb under the crook of his arm. The children were thrilled, and come to think of it, maybe it wasn't such a bad idea after all.

Now I suppose it is fair to ask why I believe snapshots like these are true, why I believe that God worries over us, and chases us, and finds us, and brings us home safe and sound. To answer that question, I would simply point to the life of the man who told the story to begin with. Some two thousand years ago, fear and hatred conspired to kill an innocent man. Jesus of Nazareth was mocked, beaten, nailed to a cross, and left to die. His disciples were hiding, his friends in utter despair. The movement that had begun with such promise apparently was over. Scholars have pointed out that if anyone should have been forgotten and lost in the pages of history, it was this man.[2] But three days later, in the ultimate cliffhanger, God gave it all back, and with the resurrection of Jesus, we learn that life, and not loss, has the last word.

Which brings me to another reason I believe all this is true: While on vacation this past summer, my daughter, Betsy, and I walked on the beach every day looking for something called "sea glass." The beaches of New England are different than ours; instead of sugar-white sand, the beach is studded with granite pebbles. Amid the mottled rocks, you can sometimes find smooth pieces of colored glass winking in the sunlight. The glass comes from picnickers who break their wine bottles on the cliffs overlooking the surf and toss them into the sea. When I first heard of this, I was shocked, because the area is environmentally conscious, but someone later explained that these broken shards are swept into the sea so that they can be transformed into something beautiful. I believe God is like that, taking the broken shards of loss and pain and giving us back something that is beautiful, something whole.

It is these little gifts, gifts of healing, restoration, forgiveness, and peace, that remind me I'm not alone in this world—or the next. It is these little gifts that remind me of how the story really goes. All is not lost; it never is. These little gifts give me reason to hope and believe. All we have to do is wait and see.

NOTES

1. Alice Camille, "Lost and Found," *U.S. Catholic* 66, no. 9 (September 2001).
   2. Ibid.

CHAPTER 12

YOU ARE BEAUTIFUL

A snapshot to show us what Jesus sees

When he noticed how the guests chose the places of honor, he told them a parable. "When you are invited by someone to a wedding banquet, do not sit down at the place of honor, in case someone more distinguished than you has been invited by your host; and the host who invited both of you may come and say to you, 'Give this person your place,' and then in disgrace you would start to take the lowest place. But when you are invited, go and sit down at the lowest place, so that when you host comes, he may say to you, 'Friend, move

up higher'; then you will be honored in the pres-
ence of all who sit at the table with you. For all
who exalt themselves will be humbled, and those
who humble themselves will be exalted."

Luke 14: 7–11

For eleven seasons, from 1982 until 1993, the television sitcom *Cheers* aired on NBC, becoming one of the most popular shows of all time. Receiving 26 Emmy awards and a record 111 nominations, this show launched the careers of actors who have now become household names, such as Ted Danson, Shelley Long, and Kelsey Grammer. The original Cheers tavern, on Beacon Street in Boston, has become a national landmark, a must-see destination for thousands of tourists. While on vacation this past summer, I photographed my children standing in front of the place "where everybody knows your name," though later I had to explain to my ten-year-old why Daddy took a picture of her in front of a bar.

What most people don't remember is that the show almost didn't survive its first season. Why, no one can say for sure, but my guess is that the show's greatest strength was almost its undoing. In a comedy market full of laugh tracks and one-liners, *Cheers* spent as much time exploring the complex relationships among people as it did on jokes. In fact, it was during this shaky first season that we find—for my money, at least—one of the most poignant and beautiful moments in television history.

The scene involved a character known as Coach (played by Nicholas Colasanto, who died after the show's third season) and his homely daughter (played by Allyce Beasley). Coach was a sweet, if somewhat addled, old bartender who longed for the good old days and saw the best in everyone, even though he got his facts wrong most of the time. In this episode, he constantly referred to his daughter as beautiful, though she knew otherwise and became determined to set the record straight. "Dad," she said, "I want you to stop. I want you look at me, not as your beautiful daughter, but as a woman. Look at me and tell me what you see."

Coach paused and looked at his daughter. His eyes grew wide, his mouth dropped open, and he said, "Oh my Lord, you look just like your mother." The daughter stamped her foot. She had made her point after all: "Like I just said Dad, Mother was not . . ." But then she stopped short. She stopped as she looked into the eyes of her father and saw what he saw. She stopped as she looked into the eyes of a man who loved a woman for more than half a century, a woman who shared his dreams, a woman who shared his life, a woman who was, for this old man, the most beautiful creature on earth. She stopped because she was ashamed to have never seen it. She finished her sentence: "Mother was not *comfortable with her beauty.*"

This scene seems like a good reflection for the fourteenth chapter of Luke, since in snapshots like this one, I wonder if others could see what Jesus saw. Here, we read that Jesus had been invited to dinner at the home of an important man, and when the guests all sat down, he told them a story. I wonder if the dinner party fell silent when they heard this parable, or stopped short when they looked into the eyes of a man who didn't see status, or power, or influence, but saw people instead. This was the point of his little story, after all, and the point of his challenge for the others to invite not just the best and brightest into their company, but the poor, the crippled, the lame, and the blind. The guests at this party had worked so hard, they were so concerned with their own place at the table, that they forgot to look around. I wonder if they were ashamed to have never seen it.

It has been said, and I agree, that most people live in two worlds. First, there is the world of work and worry, of getting ahead and paying the bills. In this world, we work hard to make our mark and secure our positions. In this world, we are rewarded when we are successful or beautiful or smart. In this world, we love a winner, and losers are pretty much left behind. To borrow a phrase from the Olympic Games, in this world, "you don't win the silver, you lose the gold."[1]

Speaking of that, I have always enjoyed watching the Olympics on television. My favorite sport is gymnastics. Honestly, I forget about gymnastics the rest of the time, but every four years, I marvel at these athletes, I learn their names, and I add their curious terms to my own lexicon. In no time at all, I find myself glued to the television, wondering aloud if one of our gymnasts will "have a good vault" or "make a stick" and beat those pesky Romanians.

But every four years, I observe something very annoying to me as well. While the athletes tumble and twirl, dazzling the rest of us mere mortals with their beauty and suspension of the laws of gravity, a voice in the background constantly picks them apart. He is the commentator, and though I know he is simply doing his job, I want to choke this guy who punctuates an otherwise beautiful floor exercise with statements like "She stepped across the line, Bob; that will be a tenth of a point deduction," or "His feet were a little far apart on that landing," or "The performance was good, but the exercise wasn't difficult enough for a medal."

Now of course, this is Olympic competition, and perfection is the goal. But if I am really honest about it, I am annoyed by the voice on the screen because it is a voice that is all too familiar. Maybe you hear it, too: the voice that tells us we really aren't good enough, or smart enough, or attractive enough, or valuable enough. This is why we work so hard, this is why we can't sleep at night, and this is why we are exhausted. At every turn, it seems we find ourselves losing a tenth of a point.

But fortunately, there is another world. This is the world of faith, the world of love, the world of redemption and second chances. In this world, we are successful when we are generous; we are attractive when we are kind. "For all who exalt themselves will be humbled," Jesus said, "and those who humble them-selves will be exalted," which is another way of saying that we don't have to work so hard and we don't have to worry so much. Jesus wanted to break that cycle because we have a place in God's universe, after all, a place of God's own doing, not our own.

In his literary masterpiece *One Hundred Years of Solitude*, Gabriel García Márquez tells the story of life in a little place called Macondo, deep in the jungles of South America.[2] It is a wonderfully imaginative book. Early in the history of this little town, the people were caught under a strange spell. No one in the village, regardless of age, was able to sleep. At first, this mass insomnia was seen as a gift; after all, there was so much work to do in building the town and never enough time to do it. But in time, the gift became a nightmare as the people realized that with the insomnia came a gradual loss of memory. In haste, they erected signs all over town so that they wouldn't forget the use of things. Everything had a label, in preparation for the time when no one could remember: *chair, clock, door, cow, goat, caladium, banana.*

In the main street entering the town, someone erected a sign that said, *God Exists.* And why would they do that? The answer is simple: Without God, we are left on our own. Without God, we are stuck in the nightmare. But there is Good News for all of God's children: The nightmare is over, and we can rest in the arms of our loving God. Look into his eyes, and see the world as it really is. Look into his eyes, and remember who you really are. Look into his eyes, and see that you are beautiful.

NOTES

1. Harold Kushner, *Living a Life That Matters* (New York: Alfred A. Knopf, 2001), 3–4.
2. Gabriel García Márquez, *One Hundred Years of Solitude* (New York: Harper & Row, 1970), 53.